# PRACTICAL
# SPELLING

*Second Edition*

NEW YORK

Library of Congress Cataloging-in-Publication Data:
   Practical spelling.—2nd ed.
      ISBN 10: 1-57685-568-6
      ISBN 13: 978-1-57685-568-3
      p. cm.
   1. English language—Orthography and spelling—Problems, exercises, etc.
I. LearningExpress (Organization). Practical spelling.
PE1145.2C37 2006
428.1'3—dc22

                                        2006046494

Printed in the United States of America

9 8 7 6 5 4 3 2 1

Second Edition

ISBN 10: 1-57685-568-6
ISBN 13: 978-1-57685-568-3

For information on LearningExpress, other LearningExpress products, or bulk
sales, please call or write to us at:
      LearningExpress
      55 Broadway
      8th Floor
      New York, NY 10006

Or visit us at:
      www.learnatest.com

# CONTENTS

# INTRODUCTION

**H**ow you greet someone depends on where you come from.

Americans use the word *hello*.

Italians use the words *buon giorno*.

Egyptians use the words *al salaam*.

The letters in the words of greeting are symbols in each native language, arranged in specific ways for successful communication. That's what spelling is. Spelling is the vehicle that carries the thoughts in your mind to paper. So, if you want to communicate your thoughts on paper for others to read, you need to spell correctly. This is true in any language.

Improving your spelling for self-improvement and professional growth is an important decision. You've made that decision; now it's time to follow through and learn the techniques you need to become a good speller.

## HOW TO USE THIS BOOK

The following are some tips that will help you use this book successfully to improve your spelling.

- Record your answers to the questions and the exercises in this book, or, particularly if this book does not belong to you, purchase a notebook just for your spelling improvement. The answers should be recorded lesson by lesson. You will be able to see your spelling skills develop as each lesson is completed.
- Obtain a dictionary. You will encounter unfamiliar words—don't let them slide by you. Reach for your dictionary, look those words up, and understand their meanings.
- Purchase a red pencil or a highlighter marker. You'll need it to circle letters and to write slash marks (/).
- Ask a friend to be your study buddy. This person will dictate words or sentences to you for spelling practice. If you have a tape recorder, be creative and make it your study buddy.
- Find a place where you can read **aloud**. Because you will be listening to yourself to identify and compare sounds, you must be comfortable reading aloud.
- Set a specific time for each lesson. You may want to set aside the same block of time each day. This commitment to yourself will keep you working consistently toward your goal.

## WHAT IS IN EACH LESSON?

Each lesson introduces ten or more spelling words, selected to help you learn each lesson's particular spelling skill or strategy.

Each Exercise 1 throughout this book instructs you to look closely at the differences in words and locate their common letters. When you see this picture of an eye-hand connection, it symbolizes looking carefully across a line of words. This is called **eyeballing the spelling words**. Sometimes, you will be instructed to circle the one word in a line that doesn't match the others. Other times, you'll be asked to circle the common letters in the remaining words. This eye-hand movement allows you to see the similarities and differences in words.

Each Exercise 2 throughout this book asks you to take a **sound inventory**. When you see this picture of an ear in this book, it symbolizes listening. To do this exercise successfully, you must read the group of words aloud because you are listening for a common sound. Your study buddy could read the words to you as you listen for the common sound. Be comfortable with reading aloud—these exercises will not be as helpful if you whisper them or simply sound them out in your head. Stating them clearly in a normal speaking voice will yield the best results.

A picture of a mirror follows some exercises in this book. This picture symbolizes **reflection**. When you see it, you should think about the exercises it appears beside. The reflection symbol also requires you to write about your thoughts. Thinking over the exercises helps you understand the new spelling skill and summarize what you have learned.

There are two exercises in each lesson that help you practice the new spelling words. This picture of a hand holding a pencil means grab that pencil and start writing! It's important to write the words as often as you can and practice writing them in context. The word *context* means to use the spelling word correctly in a sentence. Refer to the **Letter/Sound Relationship Key** (found later in this introduction) to help you remember the letters that represent the sound. If you're unsure what a word means, be sure to use your dictionary to look it up.

The lessons in this book are designed to teach you spelling skills. If you truly understand the skills, you can apply them to other words in your daily life. You'll meet new words every day. Unfortunately, there's one problem with spelling skills in the English language—they're not always consistent. As soon as you learn a spelling skill, you'll find that there are variations and exceptions to it. So just be aware that the skills don't work perfectly all the time. When you see the word **Variations** in the lesson, it means what you have just learned **is not true all the time**.

Beginning with Lesson 2, this symbol means that the nearby letter/sound relationship appears in more challenging words. Practice writing the words in your notebook and make a commitment to use them in your oral and written language.

Each lesson ends with a review and practice exercise called **What Have You Learned?** The repetition in each review reinforces the spelling skill you have learned, and the answer key at the end of the lesson allows you to check yourself and evaluate how you're doing.

## WHAT YOU MUST KNOW BEFORE LESSON 1

The English language uses an alphabet with 26 letters. The arrangement of these letters spells words that convey meaning. This book refers to the letters *a, e, i, o, u,* and sometimes *y* as **vowels**. These vowels are also called long and short vowels for the sounds they represent. The remaining letters are called **consonants**.

Each letter (or letters) represents a sound. String two or more letters together and you will write a simple word like *so* or a syllable like *de*. A syllable can be a real word or part of a word. **A word can be a word and a syllable can be a syllable only**

**if it has a vowel.** So answer this question. Can a vowel be a syllable? Of course it can, because it is a vowel. A vowel can stand alone, but a consonant cannot. The word *open* has two syllables and can be separated into two syllables like this: *o-pen*. The vowel can stand alone.

Vowels can make either a long or a short sound. Here are two general rules that apply most of the time.

1. If a vowel ends a syllable like the letter *u* in the word *music*, it usually has a long /ū/ sound. This is called an **open syllable**.

2. If a vowel sits between two consonants like the vowel letter *i* in *mu-sic* or the *i* in *lin-en* it usually has a short /ĭ/ vowel sound. This is called a **closed syllable**.

To help you hear the letter/sound relationship of the consonants and vowels within syllables or words, read the **Letter/Sound Relationship Key** that begins on page 6 out loud. The clue words on the list will help you hear the sounds. When a letter appears in italics like this, *s*, it means the **letter**. When a letter appears between slash marks like this, /s/, it means the **sound**.

## USING THE LETTER/SOUND RELATIONSHIP KEY

On the last pages of this introduction, you will see a **Letter/Sound Relationship Key** that you will be asked to refer to many times as you work through this book. The key is set up so that you can cut it out for easy reference. Of course, **if this book does not belong to you, don't cut out the pages!**

Read the consonant key and the vowel keys aloud. Listen for the sound each letter or letters make. Do this many times. You're likely to be more comfortable doing this if you're in a private, quiet place. While you're reading aloud, you need to listen to yourself and then write what you hear.

The letters you select when you write a word determine whether the word is spelled correctly. To put it another way, spelling is putting the correct letters together so others who read your writing will understand your message. Communication occurs when all writers and readers agree on the same letter/sound relationship, and using the **Letter/Sound Relationship Key** on the following pages will help you do this.

You are asked to use this letter/sound strategy many times in the exercises in this book. This strategy will enhance your ability to use sounds as a spelling skill. As an example, the letter/sound relationship for the word *rat* is /r/ă/t/. It has three sounds and three letters to represent the sound. The letter/sound relationship for the word *light* is /l/ī/t/. You can hear only three sounds in the word *light*, but there are five letters. The letters *g* and *h* are silent. Read the following list carefully for more examples of the letter/sound relationship strategy.

| | | |
|---|---|---|
| grandstand | /g/r/ă/n/d/s/t/ă/n/d/ | You hear all the letters in this word. |
| elbow | /ĕ/l/b/ō/ | You don't hear the letter *w*. |
| brave | /b/r/ā/v/ | You don't hear the letter *e*. |

This type of exercise is meant to sharpen your listening ability.

## GETTING STARTED

So you've decided to improve your spelling because you found out spelling will greatly influence what you say and how you say it. How much do you know about spelling skills? How can you build on what you already know? Asking yourself these two questions is how a learner learns. Learning is a process of construction, like building a house. Once you start, there's no end to the things you can build.

Get your tools and your notebook, and let's start the construction process!

## THE LETTER/SOUND RELATIONSHIP KEY
## Consonants

Each consonant letter represents a sound. The example, or clue word, will help you hear and remember the sound of the letter. Just say the clue word for the letter *b* is *book* because the /b/ sound is the first sound in the word *book*. This is called the letter/sound relationship. Consonants in the letter/sound relationship can appear anywhere in a word. For easy sound recognition, the clue word in the following list represents the **first** sound in the word, but the consonant can be a part of a syllable anywhere in the word.

| The Letter | Represents the Sound | Example |
|---|---|---|
| *b* | /b/ | The first sound in *book* |
| *c* | /k/ | The first sound in *cake* |
| *c* | /s/ | The first sound in *city* |
| *d* | /d/ | The first sound in *dice* |
| *f* | /f/ | The first sound in *fork* |
| *g* | /g/ | The first sound in *goat* |
| *g* | /j/ | The first sound in *giraffe* |
| *h* | /h/ | The first sound in *hamburger* |
| *j* | /j/ | The first sound in *jet* |
| *k* | /k/ | The first sound in *key* |
| *l* | /l/ | The first sound in *lemon* |
| *m* | /m/ | The first sound in *mailbox* |
| *n* | /n/ | The first sound in *needle* |
| *p* | /p/ | The first sound in *paper* |
| *q* | /k/w/ | The first sound in *quilt* |
| *r* | /r/ | The first sound in *radio* |
| *s* | /s/ | The first sound in *sun* |
| *t* | /t/ | The first sound in *telephone* |
| *v* | /v/ | The first sound in *van* |
| *w* | /w/ | The first sound in *watch* |
| *x* | /k/s/ | The first sound in *X-ray* |
| *y* | /y/ | The first sound in *yacht* |
| *z* | /z/ | The first sound in *zebra* |

When two consonants are side by side, each making their own sound, they form a **consonant blend**. There are *l* blends, *r* blends, and *s* blends. Say the word *cloud* aloud. You can hear the first two sounds. They are represented by the letters *c* and *l*. The following is a list of other sounds that represent consonant blends.

L Blends /b/l/, /c/l/, /f/l/, /g/l/, /p/l/, /s/l/
R Blends /b/r/, /c/r/, /d/r/, /f/r, /g/r/, /p/r/, /s/t/r/, /s/p/r/, /t/r/
S Blends /s/c/, /s/k/, /s/l/, /s/m/, /s/n/, /s/p/, /s/q/u/, /s/t/, /s/w/

Note that /s/l/ can be labeled either an *s* blend or an *l* blend.

## Vowels

Each vowel letter (*a, e, i, o, u,* and sometimes *y*) has a long and short sound, depending on whether the vowel is in an open or closed syllable. The combination of the letters provides a hint as to whether the vowel sound is long or short. A combination of vowel letters or a vowel with a consonant can also represent a sound. For easy sound recognition, the clue word in the following vowel key will help you hear the sound. Read this list aloud and listen for the sounds.

### Short Vowel *ă*

| The Letter | Represents the Sound | Example |
| --- | --- | --- |
| *a* | /ă/ | The first sound in *at* |
| *a* | /ă/ | The first, closed syllable in *van-ish* |

### Long Vowel *ā*

| The Letter | Represents the Sound | Example |
| --- | --- | --- |
| *a_e* | /ā/ | The word *cane* |
| *ai* | /ā/ | The word *rain* |
| *ay* | /ā/ | The word *say* |
| *ey* | /ā/ | The word *they* |
| *ei* | /ā/ | The word *eight* |
| *a* | /ā/ | The first syllable in *apron* |
| *a* | /ā/ | The first syllable in *razor* |

## Short Vowel ĕ

| The Letter | Represents the Sound | Example |
|---|---|---|
| e | /ĕ/ | The first sound in *egg* |
| e | /ĕ/ | The first, closed syllable in *relish* |

## Long Vowel ē

| The Letter | Represents the Sound | Example |
|---|---|---|
| e_e | /ē/ | The word *Pete* |
| ee | /ē/ | The word *feel* |
| ea | /ē/ | The word *seat* |
| y | /ē/ | The word *baby* |
| ie | /ē/ | The word *chief* |

## Short Vowel ĭ

| The Letter | Represents the Sound | Example |
|---|---|---|
| i | /ĭ/ | The first sound in the word *ill* |
| i | /ĭ/ | The first, closed syllable in *wizard* |

## Long Vowel ī

| The Letter | Represents the Sound | Example |
|---|---|---|
| i_e | /ī/ | The word *mine* |
| ie | /ī/ | The word *pie* |
| igh | /ī/ | The word *light* |
| y | /ī/ | The word *by* |

## Short Vowel ŏ

| The Letter | Represents the Sound | Example |
|---|---|---|
| o | /ŏ/ | The first sound in *ox* |
| o | /ŏ/ | The first, closed syllable in *model* |

## Long Vowel ō

| The Letter | Represents the Sound | Example |
|---|---|---|
| o_e | /ō/ | The word *cone* |
| oa | /ō/ | The word *coat* |
| oe | /ō/ | The word *toe* |
| ow | /ō/ | The word *snow* |
| ol | /ō/ | The word *cold* |
| oll | /ō/ | The word *roll* |
| ough | /ō/ | The word *dough* |

## Short Vowel ŭ

| The Letter | Represents the Sound | Example |
|---|---|---|
| u | /ŭ/ | The first sound in *up* |
| u | /ŭ/ | The first, closed syllable in *punish* |

## Long Vowel ū

| The Letter | Represents the Sound | Example |
|---|---|---|
| u_e | /ū/ | The word *cube* |
| ue | /ū/ | The word *blue* |
| ew | /ū/ | The word *flew* |
| ui | /ū/ | The word *fruit* |
| oo | /ū/ | The word *food* |

## PRETEST

Take the following pretest to see how many words in this book you already know how to spell and how many you need to study further. If you think the word is spelled correctly, put a check in the "Correct" column. If you think the word is spelled incorrectly, put a check in the "Incorrect" column. Check your answers against the answer key that follows. The first one has been done for you.

| Word | Correct | Incorrect |
|---|---|---|
| **1.** thum | | ✓ |
| **2.** debits | | |
| **3.** eroshun | | |
| **4.** beaty | | |
| **5.** protien | | |
| **6.** slippery | | |
| **7.** boycott | | |
| **8.** beenbag | | |
| **9.** popcorn | | |
| **10.** lotterie | | |
| **11.** county | | |
| **12.** mortar | | |
| **13.** feasant | | |
| **14.** writer | | |
| **15.** averag | | |
| **16.** eether | | |
| **17.** charmer | | |
| **18.** rythms | | |
| **19.** thankful | | |
| **20.** misteries | | |
| **21.** distastefull | | |
| **22.** sutle | | |
| **23.** cholesterol | | |
| **24.** played | | |
| **25.** poket | | |
| **26.** imitation | | |
| **27.** equipment | | |
| **28.** roufness | | |
| **29.** recover | | |
| **30.** grapephruit | | |
| **31.** lanlord | | |

| Word | Correct | Incorrect |
|---|---|---|
| **32.** reservation | | |
| **33.** lumber | | |
| **34.** karnivals | | |
| **35.** birth | | |
| **36.** starchy | | |
| **37.** emerjency | | |
| **38.** excert | | |
| **39.** shiver | | |
| **40.** progect | | |

# ANSWERS

Here are the pretest answers. Next to each word, you will find listed the lesson number in which it appears.

| Word | Correct | Incorrect |
|---|---|---|
| **1.** thum (Lesson 13) | | ✓ |
| **2.** debits (Lesson 16) | ✓ | |
| **3.** eroshun (Lesson 14) | | ✓ |
| **4.** beaty (Lesson 18) | | ✓ |
| **5.** protien (Lesson 19) | | ✓ |
| **6.** slippery (Lesson 15) | ✓ | |
| **7.** boycott (Lesson 4) | ✓ | |
| **8.** beenbag (Lesson 3) | | ✓ |
| **9.** popcorn (Lesson 2) | ✓ | |
| **10.** lotterie (Lesson 1) | | ✓ |
| **11.** county (Lesson 4) | ✓ | |
| **12.** mortar (Lesson 5) | ✓ | |
| **13.** feasant (Lesson 9) | | ✓ |
| **14.** writer (Lesson 12) | ✓ | |
| **15.** averag (Lesson 10) | | ✓ |
| **16.** eether (Lesson 8) | | ✓ |
| **17.** charmer (Lesson 7) | ✓ | |
| **18.** rythms (Lesson 12) | | ✓ |
| **19.** thankful (Lesson 8) | ✓ | |
| **20.** misteries (Lesson 15) | | ✓ |
| **21.** distastefull (Lesson 17) | | ✓ |

| Word | Correct | Incorrect |
|---|:---:|:---:|
| **22.** sutle (Lesson 18) | | ✓ |
| **23.** cholesterol (Lesson 19) | ✓ | |
| **24.** played (Lesson 16) | ✓ | |
| **25.** poket (Lesson 13) | | ✓ |
| **26.** imitation (Lesson 14) | ✓ | |
| **27.** equipment (Lesson 11) | ✓ | |
| **28.** roufness (Lesson 9) | | ✓ |
| **29.** recover (Lesson 17) | ✓ | |
| **30.** grapephruit (Lesson 3) | | ✓ |
| **31.** lanlord (Lesson 2) | | ✓ |
| **32.** reservation (Lesson 6) | ✓ | |
| **33.** lumber (Lesson 1) | ✓ | |
| **34.** karnivals (Lesson 5) | | ✓ |
| **35.** birth (Lesson 6) | ✓ | |
| **36.** starchy (Lesson 7) | ✓ | |
| **37.** emerjency (Lesson 10) | | ✓ |
| **38.** excert (Lesson 11) | | ✓ |
| **39.** shiver (Lesson 7) | ✓ | |
| **40.** progect (Lesson 15) | | ✓ |

# LESSON

# 1

# GETTING STARTED

In this lesson, you will compare words, listen for sounds, and begin to learn how to use what you already know.

 **EXERCISE 1: EYEBALLING SPELLING LIST 1**

**Directions:** Sweep your eyes across the line from left to right and back again. Do it quickly. Circle the word in each line that looks different from the others on that line.

Are you ready? Get set . . . Go!

| | | | |
|---|---|---|---|
| **1.** lottery | lottery | lottery | pottery |
| **2.** number | lumber | lumber | lumber |
| **3.** computes | computer | computer | computer |
| **4.** refine | refine | refine | refund |
| **5.** deplete | deplete | delete | deplete |
| **6.** matter | matter | matter | manner |
| **7.** remembers | embers | remembers | remembers |

| | | | |
|---|---|---|---|
| **8.** compound | compound | compound | combine |
| **9.** rebate | retrace | rebate | rebate |
| **10.** slippers | sippers | slippers | slippers |

Check your answers with the answer key at the end of this lesson.
**My score for Exercise 1 is _____ out of 10.**

## Reflection

What did you notice about yourself as your eyes moved across the line?

_____

What can you say about how the words compare to each other?

_____

If you said that there were times that all the words on the line looked the same, that's okay. This exercise is designed to make you look at words very closely, because just one letter can change the spelling and the meaning of a word. If you're going to improve your spelling ability, you must see the fine differences in words. Did you see that the words *lottery* and *pottery* are the same except for the first consonant letter? The same is true for *lumber* and *number*. Did you see that the word *deplete* has the consonant blend /p/l/ and *delete* does not?

Move on to Exercise 2, Sound Inventory, to hear the sounds in words.

## EXERCISE 2: SOUND INVENTORY

**Directions:** Listen to yourself as you read each group of words aloud. **You must read the words out loud.** There is something that the words in each group have in common. Can you hear it? If not, say the words slowly or have your study buddy read them to you.

| **Group 1** | **Group 2** | **Group 3** |
|---|---|---|
| main | feet | die |
| race | Pete | pile |
| say | be | light |
| _____ | _____ | _____ |

| **Group 4** | **Group 5** |
|---|---|
| toast | sue |
| bone | suit |
| doe | rule |
| _____ | _____ |

Take your red pencil or highlighter and circle the second letter in each word; then, write the letter on the line below each group.

> In Group 1, the common letter is *a*.
> In Group 2, the common letter is *e*.
> In Group 3, the common letter is *i*.
> In Group 4, the common letter is *o*.
> In Group 5, the common letter is *u*.

The *a*, *e*, *i*, *o*, and *u* that you circled are called **long vowels**. Read each word again and listen for the long vowel sounds.

Now look at more groups representing different sounds.

| Group 6 | Group 7 | Group 8 |
|---------|---------|---------|
| pit | mat | pest |
| lip | band | deck |
| bill | ham | bet |
| _____ | _____ | _____ |

| Group 9 | Group 10 |
|---------|----------|
| lot | puff |
| jog | jug |
| pond | numb |
| _____ | _____ |

Take your red pencil or highlighter and circle the second letter in each word; then, write the letter on the line below each group.

> In Group 1, the common letter is *i*.
> In Group 2, the common letter is *a*.
> In Group 3, the common letter is *e*.
> In Group 4, the common letter is *o*.
> In Group 5, the common letter is *u*.

The *a*, *e*, *i*, *o*, and *u* that you circled are called **short vowels**. Read each word again and listen for the short vowel sounds.

Move on to Exercise 3 to practice writing the vowels and consonants you hear.

## EXERCISE 3: PRACTICE WRITING LETTERS AND SOUNDS

**Directions:** Listen to yourself as you read each group of words aloud. **You must read the words aloud.** Write the letters that represent the sound you hear, separating them with a slash mark (/). In some cases, there will be more letters than sounds, so be careful. Use the Letter/Sound Relationship Key in the introduction to help you remember the letters and sounds. A few have been done for you.

| | | |
|---|---|---|
| **1.** base /b/ā/s/ | **11.** bone _____ | **21.** scam _____ |
| **2.** trade _____ | **12.** doe _____ | **22.** pest _____ |
| **3.** sway _____ | **13.** sue _____ | **23.** desk _____ |
| **4.** sweet s/w/ē/t | **14.** suit _____ | **24.** bet _____ |
| **5.** Pete _____ | **15.** cute _____ | **25.** lot _____ |
| **6.** be _____ | **16.** pit _____ | **26.** jog _____ |
| **7.** die /d/ī/ | **17.** slip _____ | **27.** pond _____ |
| **8.** pie _____ | **18.** bill _____ | **28.** stuff _____ |
| **9.** high _____ | **19.** mat _____ | **29.** jug _____ |
| **10.** toast _____ | **20.** grand _____ | **30.** nut _____ |

Check your answers with the answer key at the end of this lesson.
**My score for Exercise 3 is _____ out of 30.**

## REFLECTION

What did you find out about letters and sounds?

_____

What did you find out about vowels?

_____

By now, you must have realized that spelling has a great deal to do with letters and sounds. Letters and sounds have a very special relationship. There are 26 letters in the English alphabet representing more than 40 sounds. The letters *a, e, i, o, u* and sometimes *y* are called **vowels**. In Exercise 2, Sound Inventory, you practiced listening for vowel sounds. In groups 1–5, you were asked to listen for the long vowel sounds, and in groups 6–10, you were asked to listen for the short vowel sounds. In the succeeding lessons, you'll have many opportunities to learn how to use the vowel sounds to sharpen your spelling strategies.

The remaining letters in the alphabet are called **consonants**. Consonants and vowels are put together to make syllables or words. **Using the correct letters to represent sounds is spelling.**

In the lessons to follow, you will be introduced to these letters and sounds in a systematic pattern. Spelling will be made easy. The time you spend each day on these lessons will provide you with the skills you need to master the art of spelling.

Move to Exercises 4 and 5 to practice what you've learned about letters and sounds. You will review words from Spelling List 1 from the beginning of this lesson.

## EXERCISE 4: PRACTICE WRITING SPELLING LIST 1

**Directions:** Go back to Exercise 1. Look at the three words that are the same on each line. Write each of these words only once on the lines below. This would be a good time to have your study buddy dictate the words to you.

1. _____    6. _____
2. _____    7. _____
3. _____    8. _____
4. _____    9. _____
5. _____    10. _____

Consult your dictionary if the meaning of a word is unfamiliar to you.

Check your answers with the answer key at the end of this lesson.

**My score for Exercise 4 is _____ out of 10.**

## EXERCISE 5: PRACTICE WRITING SPELLING LIST 1 IN CONTEXT

**Directions:** Use the words in Exercise 4 to complete each of the following phrases. For added practice, rewrite the entire phrase in your own sentence on the provided line. The first one has been done for you.

**1.** a winning <u>lottery</u> ticket

   *The winning lottery ticket will be announced at 8:00.*

**2.** a five-dollar _____

   _____

**3.** turn on the _____

   _____

**4.** _____ your skills

   _____

**5.** always _____ my birthday

   _____

**6.** _____ the data

_____

**7.** comfortable leather _____

_____

**8.** _____ natural resources

_____

**9.** discuss this urgent _____

_____

**10.** _____ for the wooden deck

_____

Check your answers with the answer key at the end of this lesson. Only the words that go in the blanks are given since everyone will create different sentences. **My score for Exercise 5 is _____ out of 10.**

Move on to Exercise 6 to review what you have learned.

## EXERCISE 6: WHAT HAVE YOU LEARNED?

**1.** How many letters are in the English alphabet? _____

**2.** About how many sounds do those letters represent? _____

**3.** What letters represent the short vowel sounds? _____

**4.** What letters represent the long vowel sounds? _____

**5.** Write the letters that represent the sounds in the word _grow_. _____

**6.** What is the difference between the words _paddle_ and _puddle_?

_____

**7.** What is the difference between _matter_ and _manner_?

_____

For questions 8–10, how has each word changed?

**8.** matter/batter

_____

**9.** rebate/debate

_____

**10.** computer/computes

_____

Check your answers with the answer key at the end of this lesson.
**My score for Exercise 6 is _____ out of 10.**

# ANSWERS

## Exercise 1

1. pottery
2. number
3. computes
4. refund
5. delete
6. manner
7. embers
8. combine
9. retrace
10. sippers

## Exercise 3

1. /b/ā/s/
2. /t/r/ā/d/
3. /s/w/ā/
4. /s/w/ē/t/
5. /p/ē/t/
6. /b/ē/
7. /d/ī/
8. /p/ī/
9. /h/ī/
10. /t/ō/s/t/
11. /b/ō/n/
12. /d/ō/
13. /s/ū/
14. /s/ū/t/
15. /c/ū/t/
16. /p/ĭ/t/
17. /s/l/ĭ/p/
18. /b/ĭ/l/
19. /m/ă/t/
20. /g/r/ă/n/d/
21. /s/c/ă/m/
22. /p/ĕ/s/t/
23. /d/ĕ/s/k/
24. /b/ĕ/t/
25. /l/ŏ/t/
26. /j/ŏ/g/
27. /p/ŏ/n/d/
28. /s/t/ŭ/f/
29. /j/ŭ/g/
30. /n/ŭ/t/

## Exercise 4

1. lottery
2. lumber
3. computer
4. refine
5. deplete
6. matter
7. remembers
8. compound
9. rebate
10. slippers

## Exercise 5

1. lottery
2. rebate
3. computer
4. refine
5. remembers
6. compound
7. slippers
8. deplete
9. matter
10. lumber

## Exercise 6

1. 26 letters
2. more than 40 sounds
3. *a, e, i, o, u,* and sometimes *y*
4. *a, e, i, o, u,* and sometimes *y*
5. /g/r/ō/
6. The vowels (or the second letters) are different.
7. The middle consonants are different.
8. The first consonant changed.
9. The first consonant changed.
10. The last consonant changed.

# 2

# COMPOUNDING WITH SHORT VOWELS

There are many short, easy words you already know how to spell. Some longer words are composed of two or more short words; these are called **compound words**. This lesson helps you build your pool of spelling words by showing you some compound words with short vowel sounds.

## EXERCISE 1: EYEBALLING SPELLING LIST 2

**Directions:** Sweep your eyes across the line from left to right and back again. Do it quickly. Circle the word in each line that looks different from the others on that line.

Are you ready? Get set . . . Go!

| | | | |
|---|---|---|---|
| **1.** bandstand | bandstand | bandstand | handstand |
| **2.** dishpan | dishrag | dishrag | dishrag |
| **3.** handset | headset | handset | handset |
| **4.** landlord | landmine | landlord | landlord |
| **5.** bedpan | bedpan | bedbug | bedpan |
| **6.** popcorn | popcorn | popcorn | popup |
| **7.** laptop | laptop | laptops | laptop |

|  |  |  |  |
|---|---|---|---|
| **8.** hotel | hotdog | hotdog | hotdog |
| **9.** upset | setup | upset | upset |
| **10.** uplift | uplift | updraft | uplift |

Check your answers with the answer key at the end of this lesson.
**My score for Exercise 1 is _____ out of 10.**

## REFLECTION

Look carefully at the remaining three words on each line in Exercise 1. There's something similar about the way these words are put together. Can you see a pattern? _____ If so, what is the pattern? _____

_____

If you said that all the words are a combination of two words put together, you're correct. The words in this special group are called **compound words**. Compound words are two words written together to make one word. The following words are common compound words you use all the time, separated into two words. Thousands of words in the English language are compound words. They're easy to spell, especially if you use what you already know.

| eyelash | = | eye | + | lash |
|---|---|---|---|---|
| bedroom | = | bed | + | room |
| bathroom | = | bath | + | room |

Move on to Exercise 2, Sound Inventory, to hear the sounds of this lesson.

## EXERCISE 2: SOUND INVENTORY

**Directions:** Listen for a vowel sound in each group of words. Read each group of words aloud or have your study buddy read them to you. Listen for the same sound in each word. Find and circle the letter that represents the vowel sound in each word, and then write the letter on the line below each group of words that represents the sound. What can you say about the letter/sound relationship in each group?

| **Group 1** | **Group 2** | **Group 3** |
|---|---|---|
| band | bell | milk |
| pan | desk | pin |
| lap | men | print |
| _____ | _____ | _____ |

| Group 4 | Group 5 |
|---------|---------|
| top | stunt |
| stop | but |
| clog | nut |
| _____ | _____ |

In Group 1, the common letter is *a*. Can you hear the sound of the letter *a*? If you need help, break the words up into sounds using slash marks. The word *band* should look like /b/ă/n/d/. Now can you hear the sound? It has the same sound as the first sound you hear in the clue word **apple**.

In Group 2, the common letter is *e*. Can you hear the sound of the letter *e*? If you need help, break the words up into sounds using slash marks. The word *desk* should look like /d/ĕ/s/k/. Now can you hear the sound? It has the same sound as the first sound you hear in the clue word **egg**.

In Group 3, the common letter is *i*. Can you hear the sound of the letter *i*? If you need help, break the words up into sounds using slash marks. The word *milk* should look like /m/ī/l/k/. Now can you hear the sound? It has the same sound as the first sound you hear in the clue word **ill**.

In Group 4, the common letter is *o*. Can you hear the sound of the letter *o*? If you need help, break the words up into sounds using slash marks. The word *clog* should look like /c/l/ŏ/g/. Now can you hear the sound? It has the same sound as the first sound you hear in the clue word **ox**.

In Group 5, the common letter is *u*. Can you hear the sound of the letter *u*? If you need help, break the words up into sounds using slash marks. The word *nut* should look like /n/ŭ/t/. Now can you hear the sound? It has the same sound as the first sound you hear in the clue word **up**.

These sounds are referred to as **short vowel sounds**. The words *apple*, *egg*, *ill*, *ox*, and *up* are clue words to help you remember the sound. You can choose your own clue words as well.

# REFLECTION

How will the clue words help you with short vowel sounds?

_____

What is a compound word?

_____

How are compound words formed?

_____

Do you think compound words can have short vowel sounds?

_____

     Clue words can help you remember short vowel sounds. You might want to choose your own clue words instead of the preceding examples—use whatever word will help you remember the sound. A compound word is two smaller words written together as one larger word. The short vowel sounds you heard in Exercise 2 can be a part of compound words. Move on to Exercise 3 to practice using short vowels within compound words.

## EXERCISE 3: USING THE CORRECT SHORT VOWEL

**Directions:** The following is another list of commonly used compound words. A short vowel, /ă/, / ĕ/, / ĭ/, / ŏ/, or /ŭ/, is missing from each word. Write the correct short vowel to complete each word.

1. aircr _ ft
2. g _ mstone
3. treadm _ ll
4. n _ twork
5. r _ dwood
6. b _ ttlefield
7. h _ ndshake
8. l _ pstick
9. p _ thway
10. salesm _ n

11. b _ ckground
12. h _ ndwriting
13. livest _ ck
14. pean _t
15. sawd _ st
16. broadc _ st
17. headh _ nter
18. _ pscale
19. w_ bsite
20. m _ nhole

     Check your answers with the answer key at the end of this lesson.
**My score for Exercise 3 is _____ out of 20.**

## EXERCISE 4: PRACTICE WRITING SPELLING LIST 2

**Directions:** Go back to Exercise 1. Look at the three words that are the same on each line. Write each of the words that are the same only once on the lines. This would be a good time to have your study buddy dictate the words to you.

1. _____
2. _____
3. _____
4. _____
5. _____

6. _____
7. _____
8. _____
9. _____
10. _____

Consult your dictionary if the meaning of a word is unfamiliar to you.

Check your answers with the answer key at the end of this lesson.

**My score for Exercise 4 is _____ out of 10.**

## EXERCISE 5: PRACTICE SPELLING LIST 2 IN CONTEXT

**Directions:** Use any word in Exercise 4 to complete each of the following phrases. For added practice, rewrite the entire phrase in your own sentence on the provided line. The first one has been done for you.

**1.** a _bedpan_ for the patient

_The nurse provided a bedpan for the patient._

**2.** hold the _____ and dial

_____

**3.** a _____ computer

_____

**4.** music from the _____

_____

**5.** _____ about the bad news

_____

**6.** pay rent to the _____

_____

**7.** _____ your mood with music

_____

**8.** _____ at the movies

_____

**9.** use a_____ to clean

_____

**10.** eat the _____

_____

Check your answers with the answer key at the end of this lesson. Only the words that go in the blanks are given, since everyone will create different sentences.

**My score for Exercise 5 is _____ out of 10.**

## VARIATIONS

In some words, the short vowel / ĕ / (the sound you hear in the clue word *egg*) can be spelled with the letters *ea*, as in the clue word *head*. The following is a list of other words that use *ea*.

| | | | |
|---|---|---|---|
| bread | steady | ready | dead |
| wealth | health | feather | weather |
| deaf | dread | spread | sweat |
| pleasant | meant | head | |

In the following words, the short vowel / ĭ / (the sound you hear in the clue word *itch*) can be spelled with the letter *y*.

| | | |
|---|---|---|
| gypsy | gyp | sympathy |
| gymnasium | mystery | |

In some words, the letter *i* can also represent the sound of the consonant /y/ (the sound you hear in the clue word *yes*).

| | | |
|---|---|---|
| valiant | William | familiar |
| union | peculiar | brilliant |

Practice writing these variations in your notebook or have your study buddy dictate them to you.

Do you want more challenging compound words with short vowel sounds? Try these! Call on your study buddy to dictate them to you and write them in your notebook.

| | | |
|---|---|---|
| touchpad | sweatshop | sweatband |
| featherbed | breadbasket | deadbeat |
| bedspread | shoplifter | spreadsheet |

## EXERCISE 6: WHAT HAVE YOU LEARNED?

**Directions:** Go back to Exercise 1. Look at the words that are the same on each line. Write the compound words that are the same only once following blank lines, and then put a slash mark (/) between the two parts of each word. On the lines next to each word, write the letters that represent the sounds you hear. The first one is done for you. Check your answers with the answer key at the end of this lesson.

**1.** <u>band/stand</u>    <u>/b/ă/n/d/s/t/ă/n/d/</u> _____

**2.** _____

**3.** _____

**4.** _____

**5.** _____

**6.** _____

**7.** _____

**8.** _____

**9.** _____

**10.** _____

Now go back to each word and locate the vowels. Circle the vowel in each part of the compound word. Remember: The letters that represent the vowels are *a*, *e*, *i*, *o*, *u*, and sometimes *y*.

**11.** What vowel sound do you hear in the word *stamp*? _____
What clue word will help you remember the sound? _____

**12.** What vowel sound do you hear in the word *pump*? _____
What clue word will help you remember the sound? _____

**13.** What vowel sound do you hear in the word *kiss*? _____
What clue word will help you remember the sound? _____

**14.** What vowel sound do you hear in the word *elf*? _____
What clue word will help you remember the sound? _____

**15.** What vowel sound do you hear in the word *drop*? _____
What clue word will help you remember the sound? _____

**Directions:** Separate the two words in the compound words listed below. Write the two words on the lines.

**16.** pathway        _____    _____

**17.** upscale        _____    _____

**18.** redwood        _____    _____

**19.** handshake      _____    _____

**20.** gemstone       _____    _____

Check your answers with the answer key at the end of this lesson.
**My score for Exercise 6 is _____ out of 20.**

# ANSWERS

## Exercise 1
1. handstand
2. dishpan
3. headset
4. landmine
5. bedbug
6. popup
7. laptops
8. hotel
9. setup
10. updraft

## Exercise 4
1. bandstand
2. dishrag
3. handset
4. landlord
5. bedpan
6. popcorn
7. laptop
8. hotdog
9. upset
10. uplift

## Exercise 3
1. aircraft
2. gemstone
3. treadmill
4. network
5. redwood
6. battlefield
7. handshake
8. lipstick
9. pathway
10. salesman, salesmen
11. background
12. handwriting
13. livestock
14. peanut
15. sawdust
16. broadcast
17. headhunter
18. upscale
19. website
20. manhole

## Exercise 5
1. bedpan
2. handset
3. laptop
4. bandstand
5. upset
6. landlord
7. uplift
8. popcorn
9. dishrag
10. hotdog

## Exercise 6
1. band/stand /b/ă/n/d/s/t/ă/n/d/
2. dish/rag /d/ĭ/s/h/r/ă/g/
3. hand/set /h/ă/n/d/s/ĕ/t/
4. land/lord /l/ă/n/d/l/ŏ r/d/
5. bed/pan /b/ĕ/d/p/ă/n/
6. pop/corn /p/ŏ/p/k/ŏ/r/n/
7. lap/top /l/ă/p/t/ŏ/p/
8. hot/dog /h/ŏ/t/d/ŏ/g/

**9.** up/set   /ŭ/p/s/ĕ/t/

**10.** up/lift   /ŭ/p/l/ĭ/f/t/

**11.** short /ă/ as in the clue word *apple*

**12.** short /ŭ/ as in the clue word *up*

**13.** short /ĭ/ as in the clue word *ill*

**14.** short /ĕ/ as in the clue word *egg*

**15.** short /ŏ/ as in the clue word *ox*

**16.** path    way

**17.** up    scale

**18.** red    wood

**19.** hand    shake

**20.** gem    stone

# 3

# COMPOUNDING WITH LONG VOWELS

This lesson continues to expand your pool of spelling words by combining words that you already know how to spell with long vowel sound strategies.

## EXERCISE 1: EYEBALLING SPELLING LIST 3

**Directions:** Sweep your eyes across the line from left to right and back again. Do it quickly. Circle the word in each line that looks different from the others on that line.
Are you ready? Get set . . . Go!

| | | | |
|---|---|---|---|
| **1.** beanbag | beanbag | beanpole | beanbag |
| **2.** campfire | campfire | campsite | campfire |
| **3.** dewdrop | dewpoint | dewdrop | dewdrop |
| **4.** sunlight | sunlight | sunlight | midnight |
| **5.** grapenuts | grapefruit | grapefruit | grapefruit |
| **6.** rowboats | rowboat | rowboat | rowboat |
| **7.** payday | playboy | payday | payday |

|  |  |  |  |
|---|---|---|---|
| **8.** raindrops | rainfalls | raindrops | raindrops |
| **9.** keepsake | knapsack | keepsake | keepsake |
| **10.** snowfall | snowfall | snowfall | snowflake |

Check your answers with the answer key at the end of this lesson.
**My score for Exercise 1 is _____ out of 10.**

## REFLECTION

Look at the three words in each line that are the same in Exercise 1. Do you recognize the two words that make up the compound words? _____
What parts of those compound words are a challenge for you? Write any of the shorter words that give you difficulty on the following lines.

_____

_____

Move on to Exercise 2, Sound Inventory, to hear the sounds of this lesson.

## EXERCISE 2: SOUND INVENTORY

**Directions:** Read each group of words aloud or have your study buddy read them to you. Listen for a common vowel sound in each group. Write the letters that represent that sound on the lines provided.

| **Group 1** | **Group 2** | **Group 3** |
|---|---|---|
| grape /g/r/ā/p/ | easy /ē/z/ē/ | tie /t/ī/ |
| pay | stream | dye |
| rain | keep | light |
| day | Pete | line |
| sake | steamy | by |
| _____ | _____ | _____ |

| **Group 4** | **Group 5** |
|---|---|
| home /h/ō/m/ | cue /c/ū/ |
| toe | blue |
| row | food |
| boat | dew |
| code | fruit |
| _____ | _____ |

In Group 1, the common letter is *a*. Can you hear the sound of the letter *a*? Break the words into sounds using slash marks and write them next to the words. Which letters make no sound at all? _____ The sound you heard in Group 1 is the long vowel /ā/, and it makes the sound of its own name, "a." For spelling, the long vowel /ā/ can be represented by three combinations of letters—*a_e*, *ay*, and *ai*. You can use the clue word *day* to help you remember the sound.

Each of the following words is missing a long vowel /ā/ combination. Practice the long vowel /ā/ combinations of *a_e*, *ai*, and *ay* by writing them in the blank spaces. Rewrite the whole word on the line provided.

**1.** dressm _ k _ r _____    **3.** p _ _ d _ _  _____
**2.** st _ g _ coach _____    **4.** r _ _ ndrop  _____

In Group 2, the common letter is *e*. Can you hear the sound of the letter *e*? Break the words into sounds using slash marks and write them next to the words. Which letters make no sound at all? _____ The sound you heard in Group 2 is the long vowel /ē/, and it makes the sound of its own name, "e." For spelling, the long vowel /ē/ can be represented by four combinations of letters—*e_e*, *ea*, *ee*, and *y*. You can use the clue word *easy* to help you remember the sound.

Each of the following words is missing a long vowel /ē/ combination. Practice the long vowel /ē/ combinations of *e_e*, *ee*, *ea*, and *y* by writing them in the blank spaces. Rewrite the whole word on the lines provided.

**5.** m _ _ ntime  _____    **7.** potbell _  _____
**6.** str _ _ mline  _____    **8.** k _ _ psake  _____

In Group 3, the common letter is *i*. Can you hear the sound of the letter *i*? Break the words into sounds using slash marks and write them next to the words. Which letters make no sound at all? _____ The sound you heard in Group 3 is the long vowel /ī/, and it makes the sound of its own name, "i." For spelling, the long vowel /ī/ can be represented by four combinations of letters—*i_e*, *ie*, *igh*, and *y*. You can use the clue word *line* to help you remember the sound.

Each of the following words is missing a long vowel /ī/ combination. Practice the long vowel /ī/ combinations of *i_e*, *ie*, *igh*, and *y* by writing them in the blank spaces. Rewrite the whole word on the lines provided.

**9.** l _ f _ time  _____    **11.** dayl _ _ _ t  _____
**10.** b _ laws  _____    **12.** d _ _ hard  _____

In Group 4, the common letter is *o*. Can you hear the sound of the letter *o*? Break the words into sounds using slash marks and write them next to the words. Which letters make no sound at all? _____ The sound you heard in Group 4 is the long vowel /ō/, and it makes the sound of its own name, "o." For spelling, the long vowel /ō/ can be represented by four combinations of letters—*o_e*, *oe*, *ow*, and *oa*. You can use the clue word *toe* to help you remember the sound.

Each word below is missing a long vowel /ō/ combination. Practice the long vowel /ō/ combinations of *o_e*, *oe*, *ow*, and *oa* by writing them in the blank spaces. Rewrite the whole word on the lines provided.

**13.** h _ m_ work _____          **15.** st _ _ away _____
**14.** downl _ _ d _____          **16.** t _ _ nail _____

In Group 5, the common letter is *u*. Can you hear the sound of the letter *u*? Break the words into sounds using slash marks and write them next to the words. Which letters make no sound at all? _____ The sound you heard in Group 5 is the long vowel /ū/, and it makes the sound of its own name, "u." For spelling, the long vowel /ū/ can be represented by five combinations of letters—*u_e*, *ue*, *oo*, *ew*, and *ui*. You can use the clue word *blue* to help you remember the sound.

Each of the following words is missing a long vowel /ū/ combination. Practice the long vowel /ū/combinations of *u_e*, *ue*, *oo*, *ew*, and *ui* by writing them in the blank spaces. Rewrite the word on the lines provided.

**17.** fr _ _ tcake _____          **19.** aftern _ _ n _____
**18.** n _ _ spaper _____          **20.** bl _ _ print _____

# REFLECTION

What did you notice about the final letter *e* in each of the vowel combinations?

_____

_____

What can you say about the second vowel in each vowel combination?

_____

How will the clue words help you?

_____

Why is it important to remember the letter combinations for the sound?

_____

In the long vowel combinations *a_e, e_e, i_e, o_e,* and *u_e,* the final *e* is silent. The second vowel in the vowel pairs *ai, ay, ee, ea, ie, oa, oe, ue, ui,* and *oo,* is also silent. Remember this rule:

**If two vowels are a *pair*, the first vowel says its own name and the other vowel is usually silent.**

There are many exceptions to the rule, including the word *diet*. There is a vowel pair in this word, but the rule does not apply because the word has two syllables. The first syllable is open, and the vowel is a long sound. The second syllable has a vowel as the first letter, so the vowel also makes a sound. Written as two syllables, the word *diet* looks like this: *di-et*.

There are many words like this, but don't be discouraged—if you can remember the vowel pair rule, you're on your way to unlocking the secrets to becoming a great speller.

## EXERCISE 3: PRACTICE WITH COMPOUND WORDS

**Directions:** Put a slash mark (/) between the two words that make up the compound word. The first one has been done for you.

**1.** home/ward

**2.** sunlight

**3.** rowboat

**4.** payday

**5.** keepsake

**6.** dewdrop

**7.** grapefruit

**8.** tollbooth

**9.** raindrop

**10.** seafood

## EXERCISE 4: PRACTICE WRITING SPELLING LIST 3

**Directions:** Go back to Exercise 1. Look at the three words that are the same on each line. Write each of these words only once on the lines below. This would be a good time to have your study buddy dictate the words to you.

**1.** _____

**2.** _____

**3.** _____

**4.** _____

**5.** _____

**6.** _____

**7.** _____

**8.** _____

**9.** _____

**10.** _____

Consult your dictionary if the meaning of a word is unfamiliar to you.
Check your answers with the answer key at the end of this lesson.
**My score for Exercise 4 is _____ out of 10.**

## EXERCISE 5: PRACTICE SPELLING LIST 3 IN CONTEXT

**Directions:** Use any word in Exercise 4 to complete each phrase. For added practice, rewrite the entire phrase in your own sentence on the provided line. The first one has been done for you.

**1.** a _beanbag_ chair
   _Where can we buy a beanbag chair?_ _____

**2.** _____ in winter
   _____

**3.** falling _____
   _____

**4.** pick up your check on _____
   _____

**5.** a drifting _____ on a lake
   _____

**6.** gather around the _____
   _____

**7.** eating _____ for breakfast
   _____

**8.** warm, shimmering _____
   _____

**9.** a single _____ on a leaf
   _____

**10.** memories in a _____ box
   _____

Check your answers with the answer key at the end of this lesson. Only the words that go in the blanks are given, since everyone will create different sentences.
**My score for Exercise 5 is _____ out of 10.**

## VARIATIONS

In some words, the long /ā/ sound is spelled with the letters *ey*, as in the clue word *they*, and *ei*, as in the clue word **eight**. The following is a list of other words in which *ey* and *ei* spell the sound of long /ā/. Read the words aloud and circle the letter combinations in each word.

| | | |
|---|---|---|
| obey | hey | they |
| eight | weight | sleigh |
| heinous | neighbor | whey |

In some words, the long /ē/ sound is spelled with the letters *ie*, as in the clue word *piece*, and *ei*, as in the clue word **receive**. The following is a list of other words in which *ie* and *ei* spell the sound of long /ē/. Read the words aloud and circle the letter combinations in each word.

| | | |
|---|---|---|
| piece | niece | believe |
| relieve | relief | chief |
| leisure | seize | receipt |
| conceive | receive | neither |

In some words, the long /ō/ sound is spelled with the letters *ou*, as in the clue word *dough*. The following is a list of other words in which *ou* spells the sound of long /ō/. Read the words aloud and circle the letter combinations in each word.

| | | |
|---|---|---|
| dough | boulder | shoulder |

The long /ū/ sound is sometimes spelled with the letters *oo*. (See page 9 for long vowel /ū/ combinations.) However, the letters *oo* do not always have the sound as in the word *food*, *cool*, *pool*, *smooth*, and *booth*. The letters *oo* represent another sound as in the word *cook*. Here is a list of other words that make the sound as in the word *cook*. Read the words aloud and circle the letter combinations that make that sound.

| | | | |
|---|---|---|---|
| hook | book | took | look |
| crook | stood | wool | wood |
| hood | shook | woodpecker | |

The following words contain the long vowel /ō/. The letter *l* in these words signals that the *o* that precedes it will take the long vowel /ō/ sound. Read each of the following words aloud and listen for the letter *o*. Notice that it sounds like its own name. As you say each word, spell it on paper.

| | | | |
|---|---|---|---|
| sold | bold | fold | gold |
| hold | cold | mold | scold |

Practice writing these variations in your notebook. It's easier to remember them if you keep them in the same section of your notebook.

Do you want more challenging compound words with long vowel sounds? Try these! Call on your study buddy to dictate them to you as you write them in your notebook.

| | | | |
|---|---|---|---|
| bookkeeper | overweight | weightlifter | overnight |
| oversight | keyboard | honeydew | honeysuckle |
| volleyball | | | |

## EXERCISE 6: WHAT HAVE YOU LEARNED?

**Directions:** Go back to Exercise 1. Look at the words that are the same on each line. Write these compound words only once on the following blank lines; then put a slash mark (/) between the two shorter words. Next to each word, write the letters that represent the sounds you hear. The first one has been done for you.

Check your answers with the answer key at the end of this lesson.

**1.** bean/bag  /b/ē/n/b/ă/g/

**2.** _____

**3.** _____

**4.** _____

**5.** _____

**6.** _____

**7.** _____

**8.** _____

**9.** _____

**10.** _____

**11.** What long vowel sound do you hear in the word *seasick*?_____

**12.** What long vowel sound do you hear in the word *wishbone*? _____

**13.** What long vowel sound do you hear in the word *capsize*? _____

**14.** What long vowel sound do you hear in the word *cornflakes*? _____

**15.** What long vowel sound do you hear in the word *fruitcake*? _____

Which word on each line is **not** a compound word? Circle it.

**16.** delete     peanut     teaspoon     meantime
**17.** manhole     compete     pigsty     wholesale
**18.** downsize     newspaper     database     athlete
**19.** wishbone     handshake     pleasure     snakebite
**20.** holiday     daytime     railroad     sunshine

Check your answers with the answer key at the end of this lesson.
**My score for Exercise 6 is _____ out of 20.**

# ANSWERS

## Exercise 1
**1.** beanpole
**2.** campsite
**3.** dewpoint
**4.** midnight
**5.** grapenuts
**6.** rowboats
**7.** playboy
**8.** rainfalls
**9.** knapsack
**10.** snowflake
**11.** daylight
**12.** diehard
**13.** homework
**14.** download
**15.** stowaway
**16.** toenail
**17.** fruitcake
**18.** newspaper
**19.** afternoon
**20.** blueprint

## Exercise 2
**1.** dressmaker
**2.** stagecoach
**3.** payday
**4.** raindrop
**5.** meantime
**6.** streamline
**7.** potbelly
**8.** keepsake
**9.** lifetime
**10.** bylaws

## Exercise 3
**1.** home/ward
**2.** sun/light
**3.** row/boat
**4.** pay/day
**5.** keep/sake
**6.** dew/drop
**7.** grape/fruit
**8.** toll/booth
**9.** rain/drop
**10.** sea/food

## Exercise 4

1. beanbag
2. campfire
3. dewdrop
4. sunlight
5. grapefruit
6. rowboat
7. payday
8. raindrops
9. keepsake
10. snowfall

## Exercise 5

1. beanbag
2. snowfall
3. raindrops
4. payday
5. rowboat
6. campfire
7. grapefruit
8. sunlight
9. dewdrop
10. keepsake

## Exercise 6

1. bean/ bag    /b/ē/n/b/ă/g/
2. camp/fire    /k/ă/m/p/f/ī/r/
3. dew/drop    /d/ū/d/r/ŏ/p/
4. sun/light    /s/ŭ/n/l/ī/t/
5. grape/fruit    /g/r/ā/p/f/r/ū/t/
6. row/boat    /r/ō/b/ō/t/
7. pay/day    /p/ā/d/ā/
8. rain/drops    /r/ā/n/d/r/ŏ/p/s/
9. keep/sake    /k/ē/p/s/ā/k/
10. snow/fall    /s/n/ō/f/al/
11. long /ē/
12. long /ō/
13. long /ī/
14. long /ā/
15. long /ū/, long /ā/
16. delete
17. compete
18. athlete
19. pleasure
20. holiday

# LESSON 4

# PAIRING VOWELS

In Lessons 2 and 3, you learned to spell compound words with long and short vowel sounds, and were introduced to the letter/sound relationship method. In this lesson, you will meet pairs of vowels that have a unique sound and will continue to use the letter/sound relationship method. When you use these skills, more and more words will become easier for you to spell.

### EXERCISE 1: EYEBALLING SPELLING LIST 4

**Directions:** Sweep your eyes across the line from left to right and back again. Do it quickly. Circle the word in each line that looks different from the others on that line.

Are you ready? Get set . . . Go!

| | | | |
|---|---|---|---|
| **1.** pointers | pointers | pointers | painters |
| **2.** moist | moist | moist | most |
| **3.** person | poison | poison | poison |
| **4.** boycott | boycott | buoyant | boycott |
| **5.** oysters | oysters | oilers | oysters |
| **6.** announce | announce | announce | annoyance |
| **7.** county | county | county | country |

| | | | |
|---|---|---|---|
| **8.** crowd | crowd | crowed | crowd |
| **9.** prawns | pawns | pawns | pawns |
| **10.** author | author | author | audit |

Check your answers with the answer key at the end of this lesson.

**My score for Exercise 1 is _____ out of 10.**

## REFLECTION

Go back to the words that are the same on each line in Exercise 1. Find the vowel in each word. Do you notice anything about them? _____

_____

If you said that the words have pairs of vowels like *oi, oy, ou, ow, au,* and *aw* (*aw* and *ow* are exceptions because the letter *w* is not a vowel) in them, then you have a very keen eye. Go back and put a circle around the pairs of vowels.

Move on to Exercise 2, Sound Inventory, to hear the sounds of the vowel pairs in this lesson.

## EXERCISE 2: SOUND INVENTORY

**Directions:** Listen to yourself as you read each group of words aloud. **You must read the words out loud.** There's something that the letters and sounds in each group have in common. Put a circle around the vowel combinations that are the same, and then write those vowel combinations on the lines provided.

| **Group 1** | | **Group 2** | | **Group 3** | |
|---|---|---|---|---|---|
| joy | voice | out | cow | taunt | dawn |
| ploy | moist | blouse | owl | August | awning |
| oyster | point | ounce | wow | faucet | hawk |
| _____ | _____ | _____ | _____ | _____ | _____ |

In Group 1, the common letters are *oy* and *oi.* Can you hear the sound? If you need help, break the words up into sounds using slash marks. The word *joy* should look like /j/oy/ and *voice* should look like /v/oi/s/. (The letter *c* has an /s/ sound.) Now can you hear the sound? It has the same sound found in the clue phrase *Joy's voice.* The difficulty with this sound is knowing when to use *oi* and when to use *oy.* As a general rule, *oy* is written at the beginning or the end of a word and *oi* is written in the middle of the word. The common exception to the rule is the word *oil.*

In Group 2, the common letters are *ou* and *ow*. Can you hear the sound? If you need help, use slash marks to break up the words. The word *wow* should look like /w/ow/ and *cloud* should look like /c/l/ou/d/. Now can you hear the sound? It has the same sound found in the clue phrase *Wow, what a cloud!* The difficulty with this sound is knowing when to use *ou* or *ow*. There's no rule to follow in this case. The only hint is that *ou* at the end of a word looks awkward, so *ow* is usually used. See the Challenge section in this lesson for some *ou* and *ow* words you can practice.

In Group 3, the common letters are *au* and *aw*. Can you hear the sound? If you need help, break the words *taunt* and *hawk* into sounds. The word *taunt* should look like /t/au/n/t/ and *hawk* should look like /h/aw/k/. Now do you hear the sound? It has the same sound found in the clue phrase *taunting hawk*. The difficulty with this sound is knowing when to use *au* or *aw*. The only hint is that *au* at the end of a word looks awkward, so *aw* is usually used.

## REFLECTION

What pairs of vowels did you learn in this lesson? _____

How will the clue words help you? _____

_____

Why is it important to remember the letter combinations for the sound?

_____

_____

If you remember the sounds covered in this lesson as well as the letters for those sounds, you have another way to widen your pool of spelling words. Spelling is a relationship between letters and sounds, and the next exercise helps you understand this relationship.

## EXERCISE 3: PRACTICE WITH LETTER COMBINATIONS AND SOUNDS

**Directions**: Use the clue words to remind you of the letter/sound relationship. In each space, write the letter combinations from Exercise 2 to spell each word correctly.

**1.** h _ _ k

**2.** s _ _ ce

**3.** f _ _ cet

**4.** _ _ tomatic

**5.** p _ _ per

**6.** cl _ _ d

**7.** gr _ _ nd

**8.** ar _ _ se

**9.** tr _ _ t

**10.** cr _ _ n

**11.** v _ _ ce

**12.** b _ _ cott

**13.** dec _ _

**14.** m _ _ st

**15.** l _ _ alty

Check your answers with the answer key at the end of the lesson.
**My score for Exercise 3 is _____ out of 15.**

## EXERCISE 4: PRACTICE WRITING SPELLING LIST 4

**Directions**: Go back to Exercise 1. Look at the three words that are the same on each line. Write each of these words only once on the lines below. This would be a good time to have your study buddy dictate the words to you.

1. _____      6. _____
2. _____      7. _____
3. _____      8. _____
4. _____      9. _____
5. _____      10. _____

Consult your dictionary if the meaning of a word is unfamiliar to you.
Check your answers with the answer key at the end of this lesson.
**My score for Exercise 4 is _____ out of 10.**

## EXERCISE 5: PRACTICE WRITING SPELLING LIST 4 IN CONTEXT

**Directions**: Use any word in Exercise 4 to complete each phrase. For added practice, rewrite the entire phrase in your own sentence on the provided line.

1. the _____ of my favorite book

_____

2. _____ towlettes

_____

3. _____ on the half shell

_____

4. _____ and grace of a model

_____

5. _____ the results

_____

6. a citywide _____

_____

**7.** the _____ clerk's office

_____

**8.** _____ with rubber tips

_____

**9.** _____ all the gold jewelry

_____

**10.** a _____ at the bus stop

_____

Check your answers with the answer key at the end of this lesson. Only the words that go in the blanks are given, since everyone will create different sentences. **My score for Exercise 5 is _____ out of 10.**

## VARIATIONS

Sometimes when *a* precedes *l*, as in the words below, the *a* takes on the /aw/ sound. Read each of the following words aloud and notice that the sound /aw/l/ can be spelled either *al* or *all*. Circle these letters in each word.

| | | | |
|---|---|---|---|
| almost | always | already | walnut |
| halter | chalk | salt | stall |
| hallway | mall | fallen | small |

The letters *ou* are used to spell other sounds, but they are not as frequent. Read each word aloud to listen for the sound of the letters *ou* in this group. Do you hear the **long /ō/** as found in the clue word *home*?

| | | |
|---|---|---|
| thor**ou**gh | sh**ou**lder | b**ou**lder |
| d**ou**gh | th**ou**gh | p**ou**ltry |

The letters *ou* in these words make the **short /ŭ/** sound, as found in the clue word *up*.

| | | | |
|---|---|---|---|
| r**ou**gh | t**ou**gh | en**ou**gh | y**ou**ng |
| c**ou**ple | d**ou**ble | tr**ou**ble | c**ou**ntry |

The letters *ou* in these words make a **long /ū/** sound, as found in the clue word *fruit*.

| | | | |
|---|---|---|---|
| thr**ou**gh | y**ou**th | gr**ou**p | s**ou**p |

Practice writing these variations in your notebook.

Do you want more challenging words? Try these! Call on your study buddy to dictate them to you as you write them in your notebook.

| | | | |
|---|---|---|---|
| **au**tomatically | **au**thority | **Au**gust | **au**ditorium |
| s**aw**dust | appl**au**se | exh**au**st | **aw**kward |
| inst**a**llation | w**a**ltz | **a**lteration | **a**lthough |
| **a**lmost | **a**ltogether | **a**lready | sc**a**ld |
| r**ou**ter | s**ou**thbound | f**ou**ndling | comp**ou**nd |
| empl**oy**ment | ann**oy**ance | enj**oy**ment | r**oy**alty |
| rej**oi**ce | cl**oi**ster | b**oi**sterous | m**oi**sture |

## EXERCISE 6: WHAT HAVE YOU LEARNED?

**Directions:** Circle the word on each line that does **not** have the sound found in the clue phrase *taunting hawk*.

| | | | |
|---|---|---|---|
| **1.** straws | drawer | downing | dawning |
| **2.** lawn | claws | clowns | bawl |

Circle the word on each line that does **not** have the sound found in the clue phrase *Joy's voice*.

| | | | |
|---|---|---|---|
| **3.** hoists | host | spoilers | destroyers |
| **4.** boilers | broilers | employ | noses |
| **5.** coil | cool | choices | avoids |

Circle the word on each line that does **not** have the sound found in the clue phrase *Wow, what a cloud!*

| | | | |
|---|---|---|---|
| **6.** housewares | fountains | mountains | fortune |
| **7.** shots | shouts | slouch | grouch |
| **8.** bounty | beauty | scouts | grounded |

The review exercises in this book (usually Exercise 6) help you practice the letter/sound relationship method. Because knowing compound words can greatly enhance your spelling power, they are reviewed frequently throughout this book.

Which word is **not** a compound word? Circle it.

**9.** mountainside   downtown   boyfriend   noisy

**10.** cloudburst   however   lawyer   lawnmower

Check your answers with the answer key at the end of this lesson.
**My score for Exercise 6 is _____ out of 10.**

## ANSWERS

### Exercise 1

**1.** painters
**2.** most
**3.** person
**4.** buoyant
**5.** oilers
**6.** annoyance
**7.** country
**8.** crowed
**9.** prawns
**10.** audit
**13.** decoy
**14.** moist
**15.** loyalty

### Exercise 4

**1.** pointers
**2.** moist
**3.** poison
**4.** boycott
**5.** oysters
**6.** announce
**7.** county
**8.** crowd
**9.** pawns
**10.** author

### Exercise 3

**1.** hawk
**2.** sauce
**3.** faucet
**4.** automatic
**5.** pauper
**6.** cloud
**7.** ground
**8.** arouse
**9.** trout
**10.** crown
**11.** voice
**12.** boycott

### Exercise 5

**1.** author
**2.** moist
**3.** oysters
**4.** poise
**5.** announce
**6.** boycott
**7.** county

**8.** pointers

**9.** pawns

**10.** crowd

## Exercise 6

**1.** downing

**2.** clowns

**3.** host

**4.** noses

**5.** cool

**6.** fortune

**7.** shots

**8.** beauty

**9.** noisy

**10.** lawyer

## LESSON

# 5

# WHAT'S ALL THE MURMURING ABOUT?

There are still more vowel combinations to learn. This lesson introduces you to vowels that have a controlling partner. The vowel-consonant combination you'll learn about in this lesson makes a sound commonly called a *murmur* sound.

### EXERCISE 1: EYEBALLING SPELLING LIST 5

**Directions:** Sweep your eyes across the line from left to right and back again. Do it quickly. Circle the word in each line that looks different from the others on that line.

Are you ready? Get set . . . Go!

| | | | |
|---|---|---|---|
| **1.** bartend | bartend | barter | bartend |
| **2.** party | party | party | partly |
| **3.** market | market | market | marker |
| **4.** carnivals | cardinals | carnivals | carnivals |
| **5.** cargo | carton | cargo | cargo |
| **6.** bargain | bargain | bargain | barley |
| **7.** happen | harpoon | harpoon | harpoon |

|  |  |  |  |
|---|---|---|---|
| **8.** mortar | mortar | motor | mortar |
| **9.** stormy | stormy | stormy | stony |
| **10.** orphan | orphan | order | orphan |

Check your answers with the answer key at the end of this lesson.
**My score for Exercise 1 is _____ out of 10.**

## REFLECTION

Go back to the words that are the same on each line in Exercise 1. Find the **first** vowel in each word. Circle it. What letter is to the right of the first vowel? Circle that letter, too. What can you say about these letter combinations?

_____

_____

If you said that the letter *r* is next to the vowel, that's absolutely correct. The vowels covered in Lessons 5 and 6 are controlled by the letter *r*. These letter combinations have unique sounds all their own. Move on to Exercise 2, Sound Inventory, to hear the sounds of this lesson.

## EXERCISE 2: SOUND INVENTORY

**Directions:** Listen to yourself as you read each group of words aloud. **You must read the words out loud.** There's something that the letters and sounds in each group have in common. Put a circle around the letters that are the same, and then write them on the lines provided.

| **Group 1** | | **Group 2** | |
|---|---|---|---|
| art | tar | for | torn |
| ark | tart | form | born |
| cart | dark | fork | dorm |
| hard | park | corn | pork |
| _____ | | _____ | |

In Group 1, the common letters are *ar*. Can you hear the unique sound of /ar/? If you need help, break the words into sounds using slash marks. The word *cart* should be written as /c/ar/t/. Now can you hear the sound? It has the same beginning sound as found in the clue word **artist**.

In Group 2, the common letters are *or*. Can you hear the unique sound of /or/? If you need help, break the word into sounds using slash marks. The word *pork* should be written as /p/or/k/. Now can you hear the sound? It has the same sound as the beginning sound in the clue word *orbit*.

The sounds of /ar/ and /or/ belong to a special group of vowels called **murmur vowels**. The letter *r* is the vowel's partner. The vowel combined with the letter *r* makes a unique sound.

## REFLECTION

How will the clue words help you? _____

Why is it important to remember the letter combinations for the sound?

_____

_____

What letter is the vowel's partner? _____

Why do you think these vowels are called murmur vowels?

_____

_____

If you remember the sounds covered so far as well as the letters for those sounds, you have more ways to widen your pool of spelling words. Always keep in mind that spelling is a relationship between letters and sounds. The vowels in this lesson have unique sounds because of their relationship with the letter *r*. In this relationship, the vowel is **controlled** by the letter *r*. All vowels that have the letter *r* as a partner are called **murmur vowels**. They have a completely different sound than the short or long vowels you met in Lessons 2 and 3.

The next exercise will help you remember these letters and sounds.

## EXERCISE 3: PRACTICE WITH LETTER COMBINATIONS AND SOUNDS

**Directions:** Use the clue word *artist* to remind you of the letter/sound relationship. In each space, write the letter combinations to spell each word correctly. Read each group of words aloud to help you understand the letter/sound relationship.

| | | |
|---|---|---|
| **1.** h _ _vest | **6.** c _ _ go | **11.** st _ _ ve |
| **2.** h _ _ poon | **7.** reg _ _ d | **12.** _ _ gue |
| **3.** p _ _ tner | **8.** al _ _ m | **13.** _ _ my |
| **4.** p _ _ don | **9.** enl _ _ ge | **14.** rem _ _ k |
| **5.** sp _ _ kle | **10.** m _ _ vel | **15.** t _ _ get |

Use the clue word *orbit* to remind you of the letter/sound relationship. In each space, write the letter combinations to spell each word correctly. Read each group of words aloud to help you understand the letter/sound relationship.

**16.** arm _ _        **20.** _ _ chid        **24.** rep _ _ t        **28.** f _ _ mula
**17.** _ _ al         **21.** t _ _ nado      **25.** dep _ _ t        **29.** f _ _ titude
**18.** _ _ dain       **22.** t _ _ rent      **26.** n _ _ th          **30.** d _ _ mit _ _ y
**19.** _ _ ate        **23.** p _ _ t         **27.** h _ _ net

How many of these words can you spell on your own? Give it a try.

Check your answers with the answer key at the end of this lesson.

**My score for Exercise 3 is _____ out of 30.**

## EXERCISE 4: PRACTICE WRITING SPELLING LIST 5

**Directions:** Go back to Exercise 1. Look at the three words that are the same on each line. Write each of these words only once on the lines below. This would be a good time to have your study buddy dictate the words to you.

**1.** _____        **6.** _____
**2.** _____        **7.** _____
**3.** _____        **8.** _____
**4.** _____        **9.** _____
**5.** _____        **10.** _____

Consult your dictionary if the meaning of a word is unfamiliar to you.

Check your answers with the answer key at the end of this lesson.

**My score for Exercise 4 is _____ out of 10.**

## EXERCISE 5: PRACTICE WRITING SPELLING LIST 5 IN CONTEXT

**Directions:** Use any word in Exercise 4 to complete each phrase. For added practice, rewrite the entire phrase in your own sentence on the provided line.

**1.** _____ weather

_____

**2.** birthday _____

_____

**3.** _____ include fun rides

_____

**4.** loading _____ onto the ships

_____

**5.** bring the fruits to _____

_____

**6.** _____ at Club Orbit

_____

**7.** a great _____ for this brand

_____

**8.** whaling with a _____

_____

**9.** hardened _____ between the tiles

_____

**10.** an _____ since birth

_____

Check your answers with the answer key at the end of this lesson. Only the words that go in the blanks are given, since everyone will create different sentences. **My score for Exercise 5 is _____ out of 10.**

## VARIATIONS

In some words, the /or/ sound is spelled _ore_, _oor_, or _our_, as in the clue words _core_, _poor_, and _mourn_. Read each of the following words aloud and circle the letters that make the /or/ sound.

| | | | |
|---|---|---|---|
| score | store | implore | doorway |
| floor | snore | swore | spore |
| more | mourn | gore | lore |

Practice writing these variations in your notebook.

Do you want more challenging words with the /ar/ and /or/ sounds? Try these! Call on your study buddy to dictate them to you as you write them in your notebook.

| | | | |
|---|---|---|---|
| discharge | armory | article | departure |
| compartment | remarkable | regardless | transportation |
| fortitude | torrential | orchestra | normal |
| export | dormitory | organist | |

## EXERCISE 6: WHAT HAVE YOU LEARNED?

**Directions:** First read each sentence aloud. Then go back to the sentence and circle the words that have the same sound as found in the clue word *artist*. This is a good time to have your study buddy dictate the sentences to you.

**1.** The newspaper article was titled "The Garbage Barge Harvest."
**2.** The participants were discharged early in March.
**3.** The charcoal sparkled in the evening darkness.

**Directions:** First read each sentence aloud. Then go back to the sentence and circle the words that have the same sound as found in the clue word *orbit*. This is a good time to have your study buddy dictate the sentences to you.

**4.** The orchestra presented works that were far from ordinary.
**5.** The shipment of corn was transported on the cargo ship.
**6.** The oral report on the lifestyle of an organ transplant recipient was quite informative.

Which of the following words are not compound words? Circle them.

| | | | |
|---|---|---|---|
| **7.** vineyard | cardboard | hardship | ornament |
| **8.** enlargement | cornbread | yardstick | barbell |
| **9.** hardwood | dormitory | parkway | barnyard |
| **10.** carnation | hardship | sweetheart | carpetbagger |

Check your answers with the answer key at the end of this lesson.
**My score for Exercise 6 is _____ out of 10.**

# ANSWERS

## Exercise 1

1. barter
2. partly
3. marker
4. cardinals
5. carton
6. barley
7. happen
8. motor
9. stony
10. order

22. torrent
23. port
24. report
25. deport
26. north
27. hornet
28. formula
29. fortitude
30. dormitory

## Exercise 3

1. harvest
2. harpoon
3. partner
4. pardon
5. sparkle
6. cargo
7. regard
8. alarm
9. enlarge
10. marvel
11. starve
12. argue
13. army
14. remark
15. target
16. armor
17. oral
18. ordain
19. orate
20. orchid
21. tornado

## Exercise 4

1. bartend
2. party
3. market
4. carnivals
5. cargo
6. bargain
7. harpoon
8. mortar
9. stormy
10. orphan

## Exercise 5

1. stormy
2. party
3. carnivals
4. cargo
5. market
6. bartend
7. bargain
8. harpoon
9. mortar
10. orphan

## Exercise 6

1. article, Garbage, Barge, Harvest
2. participants, discharged, March
3. charcoal, sparkled, darkness
4. orchestra, ordinary (There's no mistake—the word *works* is not included. To be sure, say the word aloud and listen for the sound of the letters *or*.)
5. corn, transported
6. oral, report, organ, informative
7. ornament
8. enlargement
9. dormitory
10. carnation

# LESSON 6

# THE MURMURS CONTINUE

The murmurs continue in this lesson. The letter *r* is busy controlling the sounds of the vowels it's paired with. Spelling should become easier as you continue to apply the letter/sound relationship method to the many words you will meet in this lesson.

## EXERCISE 1: EYEBALLING SPELLING LIST 6

**Directions:** Sweep your eyes across the line from left to right and back again. Do it quickly. Circle the word in each line that looks different from the others on that line.

Are you ready? Get set . . . Go!

| | | | |
|---|---|---|---|
| **1.** certain | curtain | curtain | curtain |
| **2.** furnishes | furnishes | furnishes | finishes |
| **3.** stern | stern | stern | stir |
| **4.** vertical | vertical | virtual | vertical |
| **5.** persist | permit | permit | permit |
| **6.** reservation | reservation | reservation | revelation |
| **7.** birch | birth | birth | birth |

| | | | |
|---|---|---|---|
| **8.** purchase | purchase | purchase | perchance |
| **9.** thirsty | thirsty | thirty | thirsty |
| **10.** fertile | fertile | fertile | futile |

Check your answers with the answer key at the end of this lesson.
**My score for Exercise 1 is _____ out of 10.**

## REFLECTION

Go back to the words that are the same on each line in Exercise 1. Find the first vowel in each word. Circle it. What letter is to the right of the vowel? _____ Circle that letter, too. What can you say about these letter combinations?

_____

_____

If you said that the letter *r* is next to the first vowel, that's correct. In this lesson, the vowels *e*, *i*, and *u* are controlled by the letter *r*. These letter combinations have one sound, although it can be spelled *er*, *ir*, and *ur*. Move on to Exercise 2, Sound Inventory, to hear the sound of this lesson.

## EXERCISE 2: SOUND INVENTORY

**Directions:** Listen to yourself as you read each group of words aloud. **You must read the words out loud.** There's something that the letters and sounds in each group have in common. Put a circle around the letters that are the same in each group and then write the two letters on the lines provided.

| **Group 1** | | **Group 2** | | **Group 3** | |
|---|---|---|---|---|---|
| her | term | dirt | bird | fur | turn |
| herd | clerk | sir | stir | surf | curl |
| verse | fern | skirt | flirt | burn | burst |
| _____ | | _____ | | _____ | |

In Group 1, the common letters are *er*. Can you hear the sound of the letters *er*? The e doesn't make its usual sound—the one you hear in the clue word **egg**. In fact, you can't separate the sounds of the two letters, because e and r combine to form **one** sound. If you need help hearing this sound, use slash marks to break up the words. The word *her* should be written as /h/er/ and the word *clerk* should be written as /c/l/er/k/. Now can you hear the sound? It has the same sound as found in the clue word **nervous**.

In Group 2, the common letters are *ir*. Can you hear the sound of the letters *ir*? If you need help, use slash marks to break the words into sounds. Notice again that one sound is represented by two letters. The word *sir* should be written as /s/ir/ and the word *stir* should be written as /s/t/ir/. Now can you hear the sound? It has the same sound as found in the clue word *dirty*.

In Group 3, the common letters are *ur*. Can you hear the sound of the letters *ur*? If you need help, use slash marks to break the words into sounds. The word *fur* should be written as /f/ur/ and the word *turn* should be written as /t/ur/n/. Now can you hear the sound? It has the same sound as found in the clue word *burglar*.

## REFLECTION

Say *fur*, *sir*, and *her*. By now you must agree that all three words have the same sound. But there's an obvious difference between the words. What is the difference?

_____

_____

If you said that they use different letters to represent the /er/ sound, you're absolutely correct. The difficult part of this sound is that there's no set rule for when to use the letters *er*, *ir*, or *ur*. Use the clue phrase *nervous, dirty burglar* to help you remember that the /er/ sound is spelled *er*, *ir*, or *ur*.

Move on to the next exercise to help you remember the letters that make the sound in this lesson.

## EXERCISE 3: PRACTICE WITH LETTER COMBINATIONS AND SOUNDS

**Directions:** Use the clue phrase *nervous, dirty burglar* to remind you of the letter/sound relationship. In each space, write the letter combinations to spell each word correctly.

| nervous | dirty | burglar |
|---|---|---|
| **1.** f _ _ tile | **11.** b _ _ th | **21.** _ _ ge |
| **2.** v _ _ tical | **12.** wh _ _ ling | **22.** _ _ gent |
| **3.** p _ _ mit | **13.** c _ _ cle | **23.** b _ _ den |
| **4.** res _ _ vation | **14.** th _ _ teen | **24.** b _ _ st |
| **5.** st _ _ n | **15.** th _ _ sty | **25.** p _ _ chase |
| **6.** c _ _ tain | **16.** th _ _ ty | **26.** f _ _ nish |
| **7.** s _ _ mon | **17.** c _ _ cus | **27.** g _ _ gle |
| **8.** rev _ _ se | **18.** v _ _ tual | **28.** c _ _ tain |
| **9.** n _ _ vous | **19.** fl _ _ t | **29.** t _ _ nips |
| **10.** m _ _ ge | **20.** enc _ _ cle | **30.** j _ _ y |

Read each group of words aloud. This will help to reinforce the letter/sound relationship for you.

How many of these words can you spell on your own? This would be a good time to have your study buddy dictate the words to you.

## Using Letter/Sound Relationships

As you write the words, say the sounds in the word and think of the letters that make the sounds. By now you should be using the correct letters that make the sound. If you're doing it right, you're on your way to becoming a great speller.

## EXERCISE 4: PRACTICE WRITING SPELLING LIST 6

**Directions:** Go back to Exercise 1. Look at the three words that are the same on each line. Write each of these words only once on the lines below. This would be a good time to have your study buddy dictate the words to you.

1. _____

2. _____

3. _____

4. _____

5. _____

6. _____

7. _____

8. _____

9. _____

10. _____

Consult your dictionary if the meaning of a word is unfamiliar to you.

Check your answers with the answer key at the end of this lesson.

**My score for Exercise 4 is _____ out of 10.**

## EXERCISE 5: PRACTICE WRITING SPELLING LIST 6 IN CONTEXT

**Directions:** Use any word in Exercise 4 to complete each phrase. For added practice, rewrite the entire phrase in your own sentence on the provided line.

**1.** a _____ on a window

_____

**2.** _____ farmland

_____

**3.** a dinner _____

_____

**4.** an expensive _____

_____

**5.** _____ lines

_____

**6.** _____ of a newborn

_____

**7.** a _____ comment

_____

**8.** _____ an apartment

_____

**9.** _____ ballplayers need a drink

_____

**10.** a driver's _____

_____

Check your answers with the answer key at the end of this lesson. Only the words that go in the blanks are given, since everyone will create different sentences. **My score for Exercise 5 is _____ out of 10.**

## VARIATIONS

In some words, the /er/ sound is written with the letters *or*, as in the clue word *work*. Read each word aloud and circle the letters *or* in each word. Practice writing these words in your notebook.

| | | | |
|---|---|---|---|
| work | word | worth | worry |
| color | worship | worm | worse |
| world | attorney | | |

The following letter combinations are also controlled by the letter *r*. However, these combinations aren't as frequent, and the sound they produce is different.

| | | | |
|---|---|---|---|
| **air**port | **hair** | **fair** | **dare** |
| **care** | **bare** | **there** | **where** |
| th**eir** | **heir** | w**ear** | **bear** |

Practice writing these variations in your notebook.

Do you want more challenging words that use the /er/ sound? Try these! Call on your study buddy to dictate them to you as you write them in your notebook.

| | | | |
|---|---|---|---|
| internship | personal | personnel | customer |
| salesperson | compressor | memory | worldwide |
| worthwhile | workshop | | |

## EXERCISE 6: WHAT HAVE YOU LEARNED?

The /ur/, /ir/, and /er/ sounds in this lesson, and the /ar/ and /or/ sounds in Lesson 5 are called **murmur vowels**. All of these vowels are controlled by the letter *r* and make a unique sound. Write all the words in the following sentences that have murmur vowels in your notebook. This is a good time to have your study buddy dictate the sentences to you.

1. The torrential rains dumped thirty inches of water into the fertile valley.
2. Thirty gorgeous mermaids surrounded the surfer in the turquoise waters of Bermuda.
3. Snorkeling and surfing are adventurous water sports.
4. The German circus performers whirled on the flying trapeze.
5. The dirty water percolated through the special filters.
6. The storybook characters will be impersonated by the professional actors.
7. The patient's epidermis was destroyed by second degree burns, and the surgeon performed skin grafting.
8. Please verify the merger between the two partners.
9. There was still a murmur in the audience after the curtain opened.
10. The morning sermon reflected life in the desert in ancient times.

Check your answers with the answer key at the end of this lesson.
**My score for Exercise 6 is \_\_\_\_\_ out of 10.**

# ANSWERS

## Exercise 1

1. certain
2. finishes
3. stir
4. virtual
5. persist
6. revelation
7. birch
8. perchance
9. thirty
10. futile

22. urgent
23. burden
24. burst
25. purchase
26. furnish
27. gurgle
28. curtain
29. turnips
30. jury

## Exercise 3

1. fertile
2. vertical
3. permit
4. reservation
5. stern
6. certain
7. sermon
8. reverse
9. nervous
10. merge
11. birth
12. whirling
13. circle
14. thirteen
15. thirsty
16. thirty
17. circus
18. virtual
19. flirt
20. encircle
21. urge

## Exercise 4

1. curtain
2. furnishes
3. stern
4. vertical
5. permit
6. reservation
7. birth
8. purchase
9. thirsty
10. fertile

## Exercise 5

1. curtain
2. fertile
3. reservation
4. purchase
5. vertical
6. birth
7. stern
8. furnishes
9. thirsty
10. permit

## Exercise 6

1. torrential, thirty, water, fertile
2. thirty, gorgeous, mermaids, surrounded, surfer, turquoise, waters, Bermuda
3. snorkeling, surfing, adventurous, water, sports
4. German, circus, performers, whirled
5. dirty, water, percolated, filters
6. storybook, characters, impersonated, actors
7. epidermis, burns, surgeon, performed
8. verify, merger, partners
9. murmur, after, curtain
10. morning, sermon, desert

# LESSON

# WHAT A PAIR!

In this lesson, you will learn that two consonants can make one sound. These are called **consonant pairs**. You will also make letter/sound changes in words. This is called **substitution**. This substitution strategy will help you greatly expand your pool of spelling words.

## EXERCISE 1: EYEBALLING SPELLING LIST 7

**Directions:** Sweep your eyes across the line from left to right and back again. Do it quickly. Circle the word in each line that looks different from the others on that line.

Are you ready? Get set . . . Go!

| | | | |
|---|---|---|---|
| **1.** charmer | charmer | charmer | churner |
| **2.** style | stylish | stylish | stylish |
| **3.** shorten | shorter | shorten | shorten |
| **4.** chime | chime | chime | shine |
| **5.** starchy | stormy | starchy | starchy |
| **6.** sharp | sharp | sharp | harp |
| **7.** shiver | shiver | sliver | shiver |

| **8.** cherish | perish | cherish | cherish |
| **9.** lunch | lunch | lunch | crunch |
| **10.** ashes | ushers | ushers | ushers |

Check your answers with the answer key at the end of this lesson.
**My score for Exercise 1 is _____ out of 10.**

## REFLECTION

Go back to the words that are the same on each line in Exercise 1. Look for the letter combinations *sh* and *ch*. Circle each pair. For example, in the word *charmer*, you would circle the letters *ch*. After you circle the pairs of letters, think about where in the word the letters are located. What can you say about the locations of *sh* and *ch*? _____

_____

If you said that the letters *sh* and *ch* are located in three places, you're right. They can be written in the beginning, middle, and end of a word. Each of these pairs of letters makes a particular sound.

Move on to Exercise 2, Sound Inventory, to hear the sounds of this lesson.

## EXERCISE 2: SOUND INVENTORY

**Directions:** Listen to yourself as you read each group of words aloud. **You must read the words out loud.** There is something that the letters and sounds in each group have in common. Put a circle around the letters that are the same in each group. Next, notice the **location** of these letters. Are they located in the **beginning**, **middle**, or **end**?

**Group 1**

| shy | rush | ashes |
| shelf | brush | ashamed |
| shine | leash | membership |
| short | cash | |

**Group 2**

| chew | each | peachy |
| chop | arch | enchantment |
| chart | brunch | preacher |
| chime | coach | teacher |

In Group 1, the common letters are *sh*. Can you hear the sound of the letters *sh*? If you need help, use slash marks to break the words into sounds. The word *shy* should be written as /sh/y/ and the word *brush* should be written as /b/r/ŭ/sh/. Now can you hear the sound? It has the same sound as found in the clue word *shake*. As you can see, the letters *sh* can appear anywhere in the word.

In Group 2, the common letters are *ch*. Can you hear the sound of the letters *ch*? If you need help, use slash marks to break the words into sounds. The word *chew* should be written as /ch/ū/ and the word *chart* should be written as /ch/ar/t/. Now can you hear the sound? It has the same sound as the clue word *brunch*.

It's a good idea to go through all the words in both groups and break them into sounds using slash marks. There are many words there to help you review the sounds you've learned in Lessons 1–6.

## REFLECTION

Say *shop* and *chop* aloud. By now you realize these pairs of letters have a special relationship. In each consonant pair, there are two letters. But how many sounds does each pair make? _____ How are the **consonant pairs** different from the **consonant blends**? _____

_____

If you said that each pair of letters makes one sound, you're absolutely right! If you return to the Letter/Sound Relationship Key in the introduction, you will see that a consonant blend is two letters side by side, each with its own sound. The word *clamp* begins with the consonant blend represented by the letters *c* and *l*. You can hear both the letter *c* and the letter *l*. The same holds true for the word *stamp*. The letters *s* and *t* form a consonant blend. Each letter represents a sound. The word *champ*, however, begins with a consonant pair represented by the letters *ch*. The letters *c* and *h* do **not** each make their own sound. They are a pair of letters with one sound.

Move on to Exercise 3 to practice a substitution exercise. This kind of substitution will give you more spelling power.

## EXERCISE 3: PRACTICE WITH SUBSTITUTION

**Directions:** Change the **first** consonant or the blend (two consonants) to one of the consonant pairs you learned in this lesson. This is the substitution strategy that will help you see connections between different words. Use the clue words *shake* and *lunch* to help you remember the letter/sound pair. Write the new word beside the old one on the provided line. The first three words are done for you.

**1.** made  _____*shade*_____      **5.** game  _____

**2.** hallow  _____*shallow*_____      **6.** hilly  _____

**3.** farmer  _____*charmer*_____      **7.** brat  _____

**4.** liver  _____      **8.** brew  _____

**9.** cop    _____      **15.** slimmer _____

**10.** burn    _____      **16.** junk    _____

**11.** range    _____      **17.** lift    _____

**12.** wild    _____      **18.** scout    _____

**13.** telling    _____      **19.** poke    _____

**14.** perish    _____      **20.** by    _____

Check your answers with the answer key at the end of this lesson.

### Practice Hint

As you write the words, say the sounds in the word and think of the letters that make the sounds. By now, you should be using the correct letters that make the sound. If you're doing it right, you're on your way to becoming a great speller.

**Directions:** Now use the same substitution strategy to make changes to the consonant at the **end** of the word. Write the new word on the provided line. The first three are done for you.

**21.** dam    _dash_      **31.** run    _____

**22.** mat    _mash_      **32.** can    _____

**23.** team    _teach_      **33.** rear    _____

**24.** at    _____      **34.** mug    _____

**25.** gum    _____      **35.** churn    _____

**26.** cram    _____      **36.** mart    _____

**27.** start    _____      **37.** clam    _____

**28.** perk    _____      **38.** torn    _____

**29.** flag    _____      **39.** pork    _____

**30.** rim    _____      **40.** fig    _____

Check your answers with the answer key at the end of this lesson.

**My score for Exercise 3 is _____ out of 40.**

# EXERCISE 4: PRACTICE WRITING SPELLING LIST 7

**Directions:** Go back to Exercise 1. Look at the three words that are the same on each line. Write each of these words only once on the lines below. This would be a good time to have your study buddy dictate the words to you.

1. _____          6. _____
2. _____          7. _____
3. _____          8. _____
4. _____          9. _____
5. _____          10. _____

Consult your dictionary if the meaning of a word is unfamiliar to you.

Check your answers with the answer key at the end of this lesson.

**My score for Exercise 4 is _____ out of 10.**

# EXERCISE 5: PRACTICE WRITING SPELLING LIST 7 IN CONTEXT

**Directions:** Use any word from Exercise 1 to complete each phrase. For added practice, rewrite the entire phrase in your own sentence on the provided line.

1. _____ clothing

   _____

2. _____ in the theater

   _____

3. a wind _____

   _____

4. _____ with fear

   _____

5. snake _____

   _____

6. _____ foods

   _____

7. _____ by three inches

   _____

8. a _____ knife

   _____

**9.** _____ at a restaurant

_____

**10.** _____ your love

_____

Check your answers with the answer key at the end of this lesson. Only the words that go in the blanks are given, since everyone will create different sentences. **My score for Exercise 5 is _____ out of 10.**

## VARIATIONS

In some words, the sound /ch/ at the end of the word is spelled *tch*, as in the word *patch*. The letter *t* is silent. Practice spelling the following words that contain this /ch/ variation. Circle the letters *tch* in each word, and then write the whole word in your notebook.

| | | | |
|---|---|---|---|
| batch | hatch | latch | match |
| catch | witch | stitch | watch |
| scratch | hitch | pitch | ditch |
| switch | hutch | Dutch | sketch |
| fetch | snitch | | |

The letters *ch* also can be used to indicate the sound found in the first sound of the word *key*. Say each of the following words aloud. Circle the letters *ch* in each word and listen for the sound of /k/.

| | | |
|---|---|---|
| Christian | Christmas | chemical |
| scheduled | cholesterol | chorus |

The letters *ch* also have the sound found in the first sound in the clue word *shake*. Say each of the following words aloud. Circle the letters *ch* in each word and listen for the sound of /sh/.

| | | |
|---|---|---|
| chic | chef | chenille |
| brochure | chivalry | |

For added practice, write these words in your notebook and spell them out loud for your study buddy.

Do you want more challenging words that contain the letters *ch*? Try these! Call on your study buddy to dictate them to you as you write them in your notebook.

**chromosome     chemotherapy     cholera     chamois**

## EXERCISE 6: WHAT HAVE YOU LEARNED?

**Directions:** Write a slash mark to separate the compound words, and then circle the consonant pairs *sh* or *ch* in each word.

1. chairman
2. shipyard
3. shellfish
4. stopwatch
5. sunshine
6. matchmaker
7. watchman
8. shutout
9. quarterback
10. chalkboard
11. cheerleader
12. sheepskin
13. shoestring
14. shorthand
15. seashell
16. touchdown
17. hitchhike
18. latchkey
19. chambermaid
20. shutdown

Check your answers with the answer key at the end of this lesson.
**My score for Exercise 6 is _____ out of 20.**

## ANSWERS

### Exercise 1

1. churner
2. style
3. shorter
4. shine
5. stormy
6. harp
7. sliver
8. perish
9. crunch
10. ashes

### Exercise 3

1. shade
2. shallow
3. charmer
4. shiver
5. shame
6. chilly
7. chat
8. chew
9. shop, chop
10. churn
11. change
12. child

13. shelling
14. cherish
15. shimmer
16. chunk
17. shift
18. shout
19. choke
20. shy
21. dash
22. mash
23. teach
24. ash
25. gush
26. crash
27. starch
28. perch
29. flash
30. rich
31. rush
32. cash
33. reach
34. mush
35. church
36. march, marsh
37. clash
38. torch
39. porch
40. fish

## Exercise 4

1. charmer
2. stylish
3. shorten
4. chime
5. starchy
6. sharp
7. shiver

8. cherish
9. lunch
10. ushers

## Exercise 5

1. stylish
2. ushers
3. chime
4. shiver
5. charmer
6. starchy
7. shorten
8. sharp
9. lunch
10. cherish

## Exercise 6

1. chair/man
2. ship/yard
3. shell/fish
4. stop/watch
5. sun/shine
6. match/maker
7. watch/man
8. shut/out
9. quarter/back
10. chalk/board
11. cheer/leader
12. sheep/skin
13. shoe/string
14. short/hand
15. sea/shell
16. touch/down
17. hitch/hike
18. latch/key
19. chamber/maid
20. shut/down

# LESSON

# 8

# THE PAIRING CONTINUES . . .

In this lesson, you'll learn about two more consonant pairs—*th* and *wh*. You'll also get more practice with substitution, which will help you increase the pool of words you can spell correctly.

## EXERCISE 1: EYEBALLING SPELLING LIST 8

**Directions:** Sweep your eyes across the line from left to right and back again. Do it quickly. Circle the word in each line that looks different from the others on that line.

Are you ready? Get set . . . Go!

|  |  |  |  |
|---|---|---|---|
| **1.** whisper | whisper | whisker | whisper |
| **2.** whine | whine | whine | when |
| **3.** ether | either | either | either |
| **4.** thirty | thirty | thirsty | thirty |
| **5.** white | white | while | white |
| **6.** thimble | thimble | thimble | think |
| **7.** thankful | thankful | tankful | thankful |

| **8.** wheel | wheel | while | wheel |
| **9.** wheezing | wheezing | wheezing | wheezer |
| **10.** whenever | whatever | whatever | whatever |

Check your answers with the answer key at the end of this lesson.
**My score for Exercise 1 is _____ out of 10.**

## REFLECTION

In Lesson 7, you learned that the letters *ch* and *sh* are consonant pairs. In this lesson, there are two more consonant pairs. Go back to the words that are the same on each line in Exercise 1 and see if you can find these two pairs. Write them on the line. _____

If you said the consonant pairs are the letters *wh* and *th*, you're absolutely correct. Return to the list and circle the consonant pairs.

Move on to Exercise 2, Sound Inventory, to hear the sound of the consonant pairs.

## EXERCISE 2: SOUND INVENTORY

**Directions:** Listen to yourself as you read each group of words aloud. **You must read the words out loud.** The letters and sounds in each group have something in common. Put a circle around the letters that are the same and then write that consonant pair on the line provided.

| **Group 1** | | **Group 2** | |
| why | wheat | thin | path |
| whale | when | thank | teeth |
| whip | white | then | wither |
| _____ | | _____ | |

In Group 1, the common letters are *wh*. Can you hear the sound of the letters *wh*? If you need help, use slash marks to break the words into sounds. The word *why* should be written as /wh/ī/ (Reminder: The letter *y* has an /ī/ sound). The word *white* should be written as /wh/ī/t/. Now can you hear the sound? It has the same sound as the clue word **whisper**.

In Group 2, the common letters are *th*. Can you hear the sound of *th*? If you need help, use slash marks to break the words into sounds. The word *thin* should be written as /th/ĭ/n/ and the word *then* should be written as /th/ĕ/n/. Now can you hear the sound? It has the same sound as found in the clue words **the thinker**.

### *th* Sounds

There is a slight difference between the /th/ sound in the word *the* and the /th/ sound in the word *thinker*. Say the word *the* aloud and pay careful attention to the vibrating sound of your lips. Say the word *thinker* aloud and pay attention to how different the /th/ sound is from the /th/ in the word *the*. There is a slight difference in sound, but all you need to remember is that both sounds are represented by the letters *th*.

It's a good idea to go through all the words in Group 1 and Group 2 and break them into sounds using slash marks. There are many words there to help you review the sounds you've learned in Lessons 1–7.

## REFLECTION

The consonant pairs in this lesson are represented by the letters *wh* and *th*.
How will the clue words help you? _____
Why is it important to remember the letters of each consonant pair?

_____

_____

### Keep Practicing!

As you already know, clue words help you remember sounds. It's important to remember consonant pairs because they aren't as easy to hear as consonant blends. The next exercise will help you to reinforce the skills you learned in Lessons 1–7. Always remember this: **Spelling is the relationship between letters and sounds.** As you learn more letter/sound relationships, you'll gain more skills to help you spell words correctly. The best way to learn is to *practice, practice, practice.*

## EXERCISE 3: PRACTICE WITH SUBSTITUTION

**Directions:** Change the **first** consonant or the blend (two consonants) to one of the two consonant pairs you learned in this lesson. Use the clue words **whisper** and *thinker* to help you remember the letter/sound pair. Write the new word next to the original word on the provided line. The first three are done for you.

| | | | | |
|---|---|---|---|---|
| **1.** risk | *whisk* | | **6.** corn | _____ |
| **2.** pile | *while* | | **7.** dirty | _____ |
| **3.** wink | *think* | | **8.** sick | _____ |
| **4.** slip | _____ | | **9.** rank | _____ |
| **5.** first | _____ | | **10.** dump | _____ |

11. left    _____

12. bird    _____

13. girl    _____

14. biter    _____

15. feel    _____

Check your answers with the answer key at the end of this lesson.

**Directions:** This time, make changes to the consonant at the **end** of the word using the pairs *sh*, *ch*, and *th*. Write the new word on the provided line. The first one is done for you. Note that some words can take more than one of these endings.

1. boom    _____

2. win    _____

3. mark    _____

4. rug    _____

5. churn    _____

6. bag    _____

7. bird    _____

8. scorn    _____

9. teen    _____

10. mob    _____

11. bread    _____

12. pan    _____

13. perk    _____

14. tool    _____

15. norm    _____

Check your answers with the answer key at the end of this lesson.

**My score for Exercise 3 is _____ out of 30.**

## EXERCISE 4: PRACTICE WRITING SPELLING LIST 8

**Directions:** Go back to Exercise 1. Look at the three words that are the same on each line. Write each of these words only once on the lines below. This would be a good time to have your study buddy dictate the words to you.

1. _____

2. _____

3. _____

4. _____

5. _____

6. _____

7. _____

8. _____

9. _____

10. _____

Consult your dictionary if the meaning of a word is unfamiliar to you.

Check your answers with the answer key at the end of this lesson.

**My score for Exercise 4 is _____ out of 10.**

# EXERCISE 5: PRACTICE WRITING SPELLING LIST 8 IN CONTEXT

**Directions:** Use any word from Exercise 4 to complete each phrase. For added practice, rewrite the entire phrase in your own sentence on the provided line.

**1.** _____ for the gifts

_____

**2.** a soft _____ in my ear

_____

**3.** _____ or, neither nor

_____

**4.** coughing and _____

_____

**5.** _____ for a cold drink

_____

**6.** either black or _____

_____

**7.** _____ you want

_____

**8.** invention of the _____

_____

**9.** a needle and _____

_____

**10.** _____ and complain

_____

Check your answers with the answer key at the end of this lesson. Only the words that go in the blanks are given, since everyone will create different sentences. **My score for Exercise 5 is _____ out of 10.**

# VARIATIONS

In some words, the letters *wh* produce another sound, as found in the beginning of the word *he*. Read the following words and listen for the first sound. Practice writing these words in your notebook.

| | | |
|---|---|---|
| who | whole | wholesome |
| wholesale | whose | whom |

Do you want more challenging words that use the /wh/ and /th/ sounds? Try these! Call on your study buddy to dictate them to you as you write them in your notebook. Consult your dictionary if you are unsure of the meanings of any of these words.

| | | | |
|---|---|---|---|
| thermometer | thermostat | apathy | Sabbath |
| therapy | athletes | theatrical | thirteenth |
| whirlpool | whitewash | overwhelm | whimsical |

## EXERCISE 6: WHAT HAVE YOU LEARNED?

**Directions:** Circle all the consonant pairs (*ch*, *sh*, *th*, and *wh*) in these compound words. Then separate each word by writing the two words that make the compound word. The first one is done for you.

**1.** mushroom     *mush*     *room*

**2.** whirlwind

**3.** toothpaste

**4.** somewhere

**5.** witchcraft

**6.** toothache

**7.** wholesale

**8.** stagecoach

**9.** wishbone

**10.** whatever

**Directions:** Read each of the following sentences and write the word that has a consonant pair. This would be a good time for your study buddy to dictate the sentences to you as you write them in your notebook.

**11.** Be thankful for whatever you have.

**12.** Thanksgiving is the fourth Thursday in November.

**13.** The peppermint toothpaste is on the third shelf.

**14.** Cheers will be heard around the world for the thousands of Olympic athletes.

**15.** The chapters in his childhood revealed much pain.

**16.** Turn the wheel thirty times.

**17.** Why whisper such good news?

**18.** The stagecoach will drive north to Whisper County.

**19.** What is the path of the thunderstorm?

**20.** Either use the chopsticks or ask for a fork.

Check your answers with the answer key at the end of this lesson.

**My score for Exercise 6 is _____ out of 20.**

## ANSWERS

### Exercise 1

1. whisker
2. when
3. ether
4. thirsty
5. while
6. think
7. tankful
8. while
9. wheezer
10. whenever

### Exercise 3

1. whisk
2. while
3. think
4. whip
5. thirst
6. thorn
7. thirty
8. thick
9. thank
10. thump
11. theft
12. third
13. whirl
14. whiter
15. wheel

16. booth
17. wish, with
18. marsh, march
19. rush
20. church
21. bath, bash
22. birth, birch
23. scorch
24. teeth
25. moth
26. breath
27. path
28. perch
29. tooth
30. north

### Exercise 4

1. whisper
2. whine
3. either
4. thirty
5. white
6. thimble
7. thankful
8. wheel
9. wheezing
10. whatever

## Exercise 5

1. thankful
2. whisper
3. either
4. wheezing
5. thirsty
6. white
7. whatever
8. wheel
9. thimble
10. whine

## Exercise 6

1. mush        room
2. whirl        wind
3. tooth        paste
4. some        where
5. witch        craft
6. tooth        ache
7. whole        sale
8. stage        coach
9. wish        bone
10. what        ever
11. thankful, whatever
12. Thanksgiving, fourth, Thursday
13. the, toothpaste, third, shelf
14. cheers, the, thousands, athletes
15. the, chapters, childhood, much
16. the, wheel, thirty
17. why, whisper, such
18. the, stagecoach, north, Whisper
19. what, path, the, thunderstorm
20. either, the, chopsticks

# LESSON

# 9

# THE FINAL PAIRS

In this lesson, you will learn the last three **consonant pairs**. Believe it or not, you've already covered more than half of the letter/sound relationships! Get ready to spell more challenging words.

## EXERCISE 1: EYEBALLING SPELLING LIST 9

**Directions:** Sweep your eyes across the line from left to right and back again. Do it quickly. Circle the word in each line that looks different from the others on that line.

Are you ready? Get set . . . Go!

| | | | |
|---|---|---|---|
| **1.** pheasant | pheasant | pleasant | pheasant |
| **2.** graphite | graphite | graphite | graph |
| **3.** spears | spheres | spheres | spheres |
| **4.** phrase | phrase | phrase | phase |
| **5.** photocopy | photocopy | photocopy | photography |
| **6.** gangplank | gangplank | gangplank | gangway |
| **7.** dancing | dancing | dancing | dance |

| | | | |
|---|---|---|---|
| **8.** swinging | swinging | swinging | stinging |
| **9.** roughness | roughneck | roughneck | roughneck |
| **10.** toughen | toughen | toughen | touring |

Check your answers with the answer key at the end of this lesson.
**My score for Exercise 1 is _____ out of 10.**

## REFLECTION

In Lessons 7 and 8, you learned that the letters *ch, sh, wh,* and *th* are consonant pairs. Go back to the words that are the same on each line in Exercise 1. There are three more consonant pairs. See if you can find them and write them on the following line. _____

If you located the letters *gh, ph,* and *ng* as three more consonant pairs, you're getting very good at this. Return to the list and circle the consonant pairs, then move on to Exercise 2, Sound Inventory, to hear what they sound like.

## EXERCISE 2: SOUND INVENTORY

**Directions:** Listen to yourself as you read each group of words aloud. **You must read the words out loud.** The letters and sounds in each group have something in common. Put a circle around the letters that are the same in each group and write them on the lines provided.

| **Group 1** | | **Group 2** | |
|---|---|---|---|
| sphere | rough | bang | thanking |
| phone | cough | thing | swinging |
| graph | tough | gong | singing |
| ____ | ____ | ____ | |

In Group 1, the common letters are *ph* and *gh*. Can you hear the sound of the letters *ph* and *gh*? If you need help, use slash marks to break the words into sounds. The sound in Group 1 is represented by the letter *f*, so the word *photo* should be written /f/ō/t/ō/, and the word *rough* should be written as /r/ŭ/f/. Now can you hear the sound? It has the same sound as the letter *f* on the Letter/Sound Relationship Key and as found in the clue phrase *rough graph*.

In Group 2, the common letters are *ng*. Can you hear the sound of the letters *ng*? To help you isolate the sound, say the word *sing* aloud. Then take away the letter *s* and say *ing*. It's easier to say the sound *ng* when a vowel precedes it. Say the following *ng* examples aloud and notice that each is preceded by a short vowel sound: *ing, ang, ung, eng, ong*. It may help you to break the words into sounds. For example, the word *thing* looks like /th/i/ng/. Now can you hear the sound? It has the same sound as found in the clue word *swing*.

The consonant pair *ng*, represented by the letters /ng/, can appear in the **middle** or the **end** of the word. You will never write it as a beginning sound in the English language. As you saw in Group 1, the /f/ sound, represented by the letters *gh*, usually appears at the **end** of a word. When the letters *gh* appear at the beginning of a word, as found in the word *ghost*, they make a different sound, in this case simply the sound /g/, where the *h* is silent. The sound /f/, represented by the letters *ph*, can be found anywhere in a word.

## REFLECTION

The consonant pairs in this lesson are represented by the letters *ph*, *gh*, and *ng*. What two consonant pairs make the same sound? _____
Which consonant pair will never appear in the beginning of a word?

_____

How can clue words help you? _____

_____

The consonant pairs represented by the letters *ph* and *gh* have the same sound (except when *gh* appears at the beginning of a word and makes something other than the /f/ sound). The consonant pair represented by the letters *ng* will never appear at the beginning of a word. As you probably know by now, letters represent many sounds. In the English language, the 26-letter alphabet represents more than 40 sounds. Believe it or not, you've already studied more than half of them!

Continue your study by moving on to Exercise 3, which will reinforce the letter/sound relationships that you have learned in this lesson.

## EXERCISE 3: PRACTICE WITH SUBSTITUTION

**Directions:** Change the first consonant or the **blend** (two consonants) to the letters that represent the sound you hear in the clue word *graph*.

**1.** vase _____   **4.** tonics _____

**2.** bone _____   **5.** pleasant _____

**3.** pony _____

**Directions:** Change the **ending** consonant pair to the letters that represent the sound you hear in the clue word *swing*.

**6.** rich    _____        **9.** bath    _____

**7.** rash    _____        **10.** such    _____

**8.** path    _____

Check your answers with the answer key at the end of this lesson.

**My score for Exercise 3 is _____ out of 10.**

## EXERCISE 4: PRACTICE WRITING SPELLING LIST 9

**Directions:** Go back to Exercise 1. Look at the three words that are the same on each line. Write each of these words only once on the lines below. This would be a good time to have your study buddy dictate the words to you.

**1.** _____        **6.** _____

**2.** _____        **7.** _____

**3.** _____        **8.** _____

**4.** _____        **9.** _____

**5.** _____        **10.** _____

Consult your dictionary if the meaning of a word is unfamiliar to you.

Check your answers with the answer key at the end of this lesson.

**My score for Exercise 4 is _____ out of 10.**

## EXERCISE 5: PRACTICE WRITING SPELLING LIST 9 IN CONTEXT

**Directions:** Use any word from Exercise 4 to complete each phrase. For added practice, rewrite the entire phrase in your own sentence on the provided line.

**1.** a _____ resting in its nest

_____

**2.** _____ the rules

_____

**3.** a _____ pencil

_____

**4.** a wooden _____ on the ship

_____

**5.** roll the _____

_____

**6.** a three-word _____

_____

**7.** _____ the documents

_____

**8.** _____ back and forth

_____

**9.** a _____ hangout

_____

**10.** ballet _____

_____

Check your answers with the answer key at the end of this lesson. Only the words that go in the blanks are given, since everyone will create different sentences. **My score for Exercise 5 is _____ out of 10.**

## VARIATIONS

In only a few words, the letters *gh* at the beginning of a word sound like /g/, as in *goat*. Most of these words are related; they have to do with ghosts. Practice writing these words in your notebook.

**gh**ostly      **gh**ostwriter
**gh**astly      **gh**oulish

Do you want more challenging words that use the /f/ sound? Try these! Call on your study buddy to dictate them to you as you write them in your notebook. Consult your dictionary if you're unsure of any of the meanings of these words.

peri**ph**eral      pam**ph**let      hemis**ph**ere      trium**ph**ant
**ph**os**ph**orus      **ph**antom      cello**ph**ane      **ph**ysical
grap**h**ic      grap**h**ite

## EXERCISE 6: WHAT HAVE YOU LEARNED?

**Directions:** Circle all the consonant pairs (*ph, gh, ng*) in the following compound words; then separate each word by writing the two words that make them up. The first one is done for you.

1. fingerpaint    _finger_      _paint_
2. fingernail    _____      _____
3. singsong    _____      _____
4. singlehanded    _____      _____
5. roughneck    _____      _____
6. speakerphone    _____      _____
7. ringleader    _____      _____
8. ringworm    _____      _____
9. ringmaster    _____      _____
10. fingerprint    _____      _____

**Directions:** Read each of the following sentences and write the words that have a consonant pair you have learned. This would be a good time for your study buddy to dictate the sentences to you as you write them in your notebook.

11. The Philadelphia Philharmonic will perform on the first Thursday in March.
12. Unknowingly, the pheasants posed for the photographer.
13. Three gongs mean to leave right away.
14. Bang on the door three times and I will let you in.
15. The Earth is shaped like a sphere.
16. Can you phrase that one more time?
17. Draw the lines on the graph with a red pen.
18. The pendulum swings back and forth.
19. Ring the phone three times and then hang up.
20. Tell us the truth about the phantom.

Check your answers with the answer key at the end of this lesson.
**My score for Exercise 6 is _____ out of 20.**

# ANSWERS

## Exercise 1

1. pleasant
2. graph
3. spears
4. phase
5. photography
6. gangway
7. dance
8. stinging
9. roughness
10. touring

## Exercise 3

1. phase
2. phone
3. phony
4. phonics
5. pheasant
6. ring
7. rang
8. pang
9. bang
10. sung

## Exercise 4

1. pheasant
2. graphite
3. spheres
4. phrase
5. photocopy
6. gangplank
7. dancing
8. swinging
9. roughneck
10. toughen

## Exercise 5

1. pheasant
2. toughen
3. graphite
4. gangplank
5. sphere
6. phrase
7. photocopy
8. swinging
9. roughneck
10. dancing

## Exercise 6

1. finger    paint
2. finger    nail
3. sing    song
4. single    handed
5. rough    neck
6. speaker    phone
7. ring    leader
8. ring    worm
9. ring    master
10. finger    print
11. the, Philadelphia, Philharmonic, Thursday, March
12. unknowingly, the, pheasants, photographer
13. three, gongs (There is no mistake; the word *right* does not belong here. See Lesson 3.)
14. bang, the, three
15. the, Earth, shaped, sphere
16. phrase, that
17. the, graph, with
18. the, swings, forth
19. ring, the, phone, three, then, hang
20. truth, the, phantom

# LESSON

# 10

# THE SOFTENING OF CONSONANTS

So far, you have learned that each consonant has only one sound. However, in this lesson, you'll see that some consonants have two sounds. To differentiate between the two sounds, one will be called **hard** and the other will be called **soft**.

## EXERCISE 1: EYEBALLING SPELLING LIST 10

**Directions:** Sweep your eyes across the line from left to right and back again. Do it quickly. Circle the word in each line that looks different from the others on that line.

Are you ready? Get set . . . Go!

| | | | |
|---|---|---|---|
| **1.** celebrate | celebrate | celibate | celebrate |
| **2.** cellular | cellular | cellular | celluloid |
| **3.** palace | place | palace | palace |
| **4.** centerpiece | centerpiece | centerpiece | certainty |
| **5.** century | century | century | censor |
| **6.** refrigerator | regenerator | refrigerator | refrigerator |
| **7.** average | average | acreage | average |

| **8.** germs | gems | gems | gems |
| **9.** emergency | emergency | emergency | emerge |
| **10.** agents | agents | angels | agents |

Check your answers with the answer key at the end of this lesson.
**My score for Exercise 1 is _____ out of 10.**

## REFLECTION

Go back to the words that are the same on each line in Exercise 1. Locate the letters *c* and *g*. What kind of letter follows the letters *c* and *g*?

_____

You should have seen that a vowel always follows the letters *c* and *g* in the words above. Vowels are the only clue for understanding the concept of two sounds for one consonant. Move on to Exercise 2, Sound Inventory, to hear the sounds in this lesson.

## EXERCISE 2: SOUND INVENTORY

**Directions:** Listen to yourself as you read each group of words aloud. **You must read the words out loud.** The letters and sounds in each group have something in common. Put a circle around the letters that are the same in each group and then write them on the lines provided.

**Group 1**

| cell | voice |
| city | lacy |
| cent | recite |

_____

**Group 2**

| cake | music |
| cord | magic |
| cub | act |

_____

**Group 3**

| gems | agent |
| germs | angel |
| gist | cage |

_____

**Group 4**

| girl | ugly |
| grow | beg |
| grass | rug |

_____

In Group 1, the common letter is *c*. Can you hear the sound of the letter *c*? If you need help, use slash marks to break the words into sounds. The sound in Group 1 is the same as the letter *s*, so the word *city* should be written /s/ ĭ /t/ē/. This sound is called the **soft** sound of the letter *c*. It has the same sound as the letter *s* on the Letter/Sound Relationship Key and as the letter *c* in the clue word *celery*.

In Group 2, the common letter is also *c*. Can you hear the sound of this letter *c*? If you need help, use slash marks to break the words into sounds using the letter/sound strategy. The sound in Group 2 is the same as the letter *k*, so the word *cake* should be written /k/ā/k/. This sound is called the **hard** sound of the letter *c*. It has the same sound as the letter *k* on the Letter/Sound Relationship Key and as found in the clue word *cake*.

In Group 3, the common letter is *g*. Can you hear the sound of the letter *g*? If you need help, use slash marks to break the words into sounds using the letter/sound strategy. The sound in Group 3 is the same as the letter *j*, so the word *gems* should be written /j/ ĕ /m/s/. This sound is called the **soft** sound of the letter *g*. It has the same sound as the letter *j* on the Letter/Sound Relationship Key and as found in the clue word **George**.

In Group 4, the common letter is also *g*. Can you hear the sound of this letter *g*? If you need help, use slash marks to break the words into sounds. The sound in Group 4 is the same as the letter *g*, so the word *gate* should be written /g/ā/t/. This sound is called the **hard** sound of the letter *g*. It has the same sound as the letter *g* on the Letter/Sound Relationship Key and as found in the clue word *goat*.

# REFLECTION

What consonants did you learn about in this lesson? _____

What can you say about the sounds of the consonants?

_____

_____

What will help you decide whether a sound is soft or hard?

_____

The consonants in this lesson are the letters *c* and *g*. The letter *c* has a soft and hard sound, and the letter *g* has a soft and hard sound. The following is a general rule:

> **If either *e* or *i* follows the consonant *c* or *g*, the sound is *usually* (but not always) soft.**

For practice with the soft consonants, move on to Exercise 3.

## EXERCISE 3: PRACTICE WITH SUBSTITUTION

**Directions:** Change the first consonant to the sound of soft *c*.

**1.** dent     _____     **4.** renter     _____

**2.** pity     _____     **5.** lease     _____

**3.** bell     _____

**Directions:** Change the first consonant to the soft sound of *g*.

**6.** venerate     _____     **9.** lender     _____

**7.** term     _____     **10.** terminate     _____

**8.** list     _____

Check your answers with the answer key at the end of this lesson.
**My score for Exercise 3 is _____ out of 10.**

## EXERCISE 4: PRACTICE WRITING SPELLING LIST 10

**Directions:** Go back to Exercise 1. Look at the three words that are the same on each line. Write each of these words only once on the lines below. This would be a good time to have your study buddy dictate the words to you.

**1.** _____      **6.** _____

**2.** _____      **7.** _____

**3.** _____      **8.** _____

**4.** _____      **9.** _____

**5.** _____      **10.** _____

Consult your dictionary if the meaning of a word is unfamiliar to you.

Check your answers with the answer key at the end of this lesson.

**My score for Exercise 4 is _____ out of 10.**

## EXERCISE 5: PRACTICE WRITING SPELLING LIST 10 IN CONTEXT

**Directions:** Use any word from Exercise 4 to complete each phrase. For added practice, rewrite the entire phrase in your own sentence on the provided line.

**1.** insurance _____

_____

**2.** _____ exit

_____

**3.** _____ a holiday

_____

**4.** the twentieth _____

_____

**5.** a _____ phone

_____

**6.** shiny _____ in a necklace

_____

**7.** the _____ score

_____

**8.** milk in the _____

_____

**9.** a flowering _____

_____

**10.** a king's _____

_____

Check your answers with the answer key at the end of this lesson. Only the words that go in the blanks are given, since everyone will create different sentences. **My score for Exercise 5 is _____ out of 10.**

## VARIATIONS

In some words, the letters *ge* are preceded by the letter *d*, as in the word *judge*. In such words, the consonant letter *g* is a soft sound and the letter *d* is silent. Circle the letters *dge* in each word. Practice writing them or have your study buddy dictate them to you.

| | | | |
|---|---|---|---|
| judge | fudge | budge | ridge |
| bridge | wedge | hedge | pledge |
| ledge | badge | edge | lodge |
| sludge | smudge | grudge | |

A few common words, including *girl*, *get*, and *gimmick*, have a hard /g/ sound even though they have *e* or *i* after the *g*.

Do you want more challenging words that use the /c/ and /g/ sounds? Try these! Call on your study buddy to dictate them to you as you write them in your notebook. Consult your dictionary if you need to so that you can use the words correctly.

| | | | |
|---|---|---|---|
| cylinder | ceiling | innocent | civility |
| cement | December | decimate | voiceless |
| process | recess | spicy | cemetery |
| | | | |
| tragedy | general | genocide | generate |
| Germany | generosity | plunger | revenge |
| gelatin | germicidal | refrigerator | |

## EXERCISE 6: WHAT HAVE YOU LEARNED?

**Directions:** Use words from Exercise 4 to complete the following sentences.

**1.** Which word means a period of 100 years? _____

**2.** Which word means a person who is a representative?

_____

**3.** Which word means a decoration for the center of a table?

_____

**4.** Which word means precious stones? _____

**5.** Which word means a kind of phone? _____

**Directions:** Complete each sentence by choosing one word.

**6.** When will you _____ your next birthday? (celebrate, celibate)

**7.** The agent's _____ rang endlessly. (cellophane, cellular phone)

**8.** The gypsy performed _____, and the man was healed. (manic, magic)

**9.** The Queen of England resides at Buckingham _____. (Palace, Place)

**10.** The _____ meeting will be held in the center hall. (lodge, ledge)

**Directions:** Circle all the words in the following sentences that have a soft *c* and/or *g*.

**11.** Add cinnamon spice to the hot apple cider.

**12.** Cement is a process developed by the ancient Romans.

**13.** The ceilings in the palace were painted with gold leaf.

**14.** The death of the general is truly a tragedy.

**15.** Gelatin is easy to digest.

**16.** It is too cold for the seeds to germinate in December.

**17.** That baby has such an angelic face.

**18.** It is too cool in the cellar to store the spices there.

**19.** The police officer's badge was removed by the judge.

**20.** Recite the Pledge of Allegiance.

**Directions:** Separate the words you circled in sentences 11–20 by putting all the soft *c* words in one column and all the soft *g* words in the other column.

**Words with Soft *c***

_____

_____

_____

_____

_____

**Words with Soft *g***

_____

_____

_____

_____

_____

Check your answers with the answer key at the end of this lesson.

**My score for Exercise 6 is _____ out of 20.**

# ANSWERS

## Exercise 1

**1.** celibate
**2.** celluloid
**3.** place
**4.** certainty
**5.** censor
**6.** regenerator
**7.** acreage
**8.** germs
**9.** emerge
**10.** angels

## Exercise 3

**1.** cent
**2.** city
**3.** cell
**4.** center
**5.** cease
**6.** generate
**7.** germ
**8.** gist
**9.** gender
**10.** germinate

## Exercise 4

1. celebrate
2. cellular
3. palace
4. centerpiece
5. century
6. refrigerator
7. average
8. gems
9. emergency
10. agents

## Exercise 5

1. agents
2. emergency
3. celebrate
4. century
5. cellular
6. gems
7. average
8. refrigerator
9. centerpiece
10. palace

## Exercise 6

1. century
2. agent
3. centerpiece
4. gems
5. cellular
6. celebrate
7. cellular phone
8. magic
9. Palace
10. lodge
11. cinnamon, spice, cider
12. cement, process, ancient
13. ceilings, palace
14. general, tragedy
15. gelatin, digest
16. germinate, December
17. angelic, face
18. cellar, spices
19. police, officer's, badge, judge
20. recite, Pledge, Allegiance

## Words with Soft *c*

cinnamon
spice
cider
cement
process
ceilings
palace
December
face
cellar
spices
police
recite
officer's
ancient

## Words with Soft *g*

general
tragedy
gelatin
digest
germinate
angelic
badge
judge
pledge
Allegiance

# LESSON

# 11

# THE ODDBALL CONSONANTS

The consonants in this lesson have unusual letter/sound relationships. That's why we call them the "oddball consonants." When you finish this lesson, you will be familiar with the special spelling strategies involving the letters *x* and *q*.

## EXERCISE 1: EYEBALLING SPELLING LIST 11

**Directions:** Sweep your eyes across the line from left to right and back again. Do it quickly. Circle the word in each line that looks different from the others on that line.

Are you ready? Get set . . . Go!

| | | | |
|---|---|---|---|
| **1.** quit | quit | quit | quilt |
| **2.** quill | quill | quill | quip |
| **3.** quality | qualify | qualify | qualify |
| **4.** equipment | equipment | equipment | equality |
| **5.** sequels | sequels | sequins | sequels |
| **6.** sixty | sticky | sixty | sixty |
| **7.** excerpt | excerpt | excerpt | except |

| | | | |
|---|---|---|---|
| **8.** exact | exact | exult | exact |
| **9.** explore | explore | explore | expose |
| **10.** extract | extract | exact | extract |

Check your answers with the answer key at the end of this lesson.
**My score for Exercise 1 is _____ out of 10.**

## REFLECTION

Go back to the words that are the same on each line in Exercise 1. Locate the letters *x* and *q*. Each of these letters has a partner.

What letter is the partner of the letter *x*?    _____
What letter is the partner of the letter *q*?    _____

The letter *x* usually has the letter *e* or another vowel as a partner, and the letter *q* always has the letter *u* as a partner. The unusual thing about these letters is their sound. Move on to Exercise 2, Sound Inventory, to hear the sounds of these oddball consonants.

## EXERCISE 2: SOUND INVENTORY

**Directions:** Listen to yourself as you read each group of words aloud. **You must read the words out loud.** The letters and sounds in each group have something in common. Put a circle around the letters that are the same in each group and then write them on the lines provided.

| Group 1 | Group 2 | Group 3 |
|---|---|---|
| quit | exit | box |
| queen | explode | six |
| quick | exist | fox |
| quack | extend | tax |
| _____ | _____ | _____ |

In Group 1, the common letters are *qu*. Can you hear the sound of the letters *qu*? If you need help, use slash marks to break the words into sounds. The word *quit* should be written as /k/w/ĭ/t/ and the word *queen* should be written as k/w/ē/n/. Now can you hear the sound? The letters *qu* represent the combined sound of /k/ and /w/, as found in the clue word **quilt**.

In Group 2, the common letters are *ex*. Can you hear the sound of the letters *ex*? If you need help, use slash marks to break the words into sounds. The word *exit* should be written as / ĕ /k/s/ ĭ /t/ and the word *extend* should be written as / ĕ /k/s/t/ ĕ /n/d/. Now can you hear the sound? The letters *ex* represent the sound of the combination / ĕ /k/s/, as found in the clue word **ex**tract.

In Group 3, the common letter is *x*. Can you hear the sound of the letter *x*? If you need help, use slash marks to break the words into sounds. The word *box* should be written as /b/ŏ/k/s/ and the word *tax* should be written as /t/ă/k/s/. Now can you hear the sound? The letter *x* represents the sound of the two consonants /k/s/ as found in the clue word **ex**tract.

## REFLECTION

What consonants did you learn about in this lesson? _____

What sounds do these consonants represent? _____

Why are these consonants called the oddball consonants? _____

_____

The consonants in this lesson are represented by the letters *qu* and *x*. The letters *qu* represent the sound of /k/w/ and the letter *x* represents the sound of /k/s/. If the letter *e* precedes the letter *x*, you hear a syllable that sounds like /ĕ/k/s/.

These consonants are called the oddball consonants because they have strange letter/sound relationships. The letter *x*, a single consonant, makes two sounds: /k/s/. The consonant letter *q* is **always** followed by the letter *u* and together they make the sound /k/w/. For practice with these consonants, move on to Exercise 3.

## EXERCISE 3: PRACTICE WITH SUBSTITUTION

**Directions:** Change the first consonant in each word to the vowel/consonant combination you hear in the beginning of the word **ex**tract. The first one is done for you.

**1.** sit      _____*exit*_____      **4.** fist      _____

**2.** pact      _____      **5.** fit      _____

**3.** mile      _____

**Directions:** Change the first consonant in each word to the consonant/vowel combination you hear in the beginning of the word **qu**ilt. The first one is done for you.

**6.** bit      _____*quit*_____      **9.** paint      _____

**7.** rail      _____      **10.** river      _____

**8.** teen      _____

**Directions:** Change the first consonant(s) in each word to the consonant/vowel combination you hear in the word *squirt*. The first one is done for you.

**11.** leaky     _____*squeaky*_____     **14.** freeze     _____

**12.** dirt     _____     **15.** deal     _____

**13.** hint     _____

**Directions:** Change the final consonant to the letter *x*.

**16.** sin     _____*six*_____     **19.** tap     _____

**17.** wag     _____     **20.** fat     _____

**18.** fog     _____

Check your answers with the answer key at the end of this lesson.
**My score for Exercise 3 is _____ out of 20.**

## EXERCISE 4: PRACTICE WRITING SPELLING LIST 11

**Directions:** Go back to Exercise 1. Look at the three words that are the same on each line. Write each of these words only once on the lines below. This would be a good time to have your study buddy dictate the words to you.

**1.** _____     **6.** _____

**2.** _____     **7.** _____

**3.** _____     **8.** _____

**4.** _____     **9.** _____

**5.** _____     **10.** _____

Consult your dictionary if the meaning of a word is unfamiliar to you. Check your answers with the answer key at the end of this lesson.
**My score for Exercise 4 is _____ out of 10.**

## EXERCISE 5: PRACTICE WRITING SPELLING LIST 11 IN CONTEXT

**Directions:** Use any word from Exercise 4 to complete each phrase. For added practice, rewrite the entire phrase in your own sentence on the provided line.

**1.** lemon _____ for flavoring

_____

**2.** _____ a job

_____

**3.** a _____ and ink

_____

**4.** _____ the unknown

_____

**5.** _____ for the position

_____

**6.** add the _____ amount

_____

**7.** tools and _____

_____

**8.** an _____ from a book

_____

**9.** two _____ to the movie

_____

**10.** _____ years old

_____

Check your answers with the answer key at the end of this lesson. Only the words that go in the blanks are given, since everyone will create different sentences. **My score for Exercise 5 is _____ out of 10.**

Do you want more challenging words that contain the letters *x* and *qu*? Try these! Call on your study buddy to dictate them to you as you write them in your notebook. Consult your dictionary if necessary so that you can use the words correctly.

| | | | |
|---|---|---|---|
| exonerate | exhibit | expensive | experiment |
| except | exhale | expound | exploit |
| external | expect | exceed | exchange |
| existence | extraction | exercise | oxide |
| fixate | sixteenth | oxygen | |

| | | | |
|---|---|---|---|
| **qu**icksand | se**qu**ence | a**qu**atic | **qu**intet |
| **qu**iet | **qu**ite | | |

## EXERCISE 6: WHAT HAVE YOU LEARNED?

In Lesson 10, you learned about the softening of the consonants *c* and *g*. In this lesson, you learned about the oddball consonants *x* and *qu*. The next exercise reviews all of these spelling skills.

**Directions:** Read each compound word aloud. Rewrite each compound word as two words on the lines provided.

**1.** gentleman _____ _____

**2.** expressway _____ _____

**3.** taxpayer _____ _____

**4.** bridgework _____ _____

**5.** facelift _____ _____

**6.** pacemaker _____ _____

**7.** policeman _____ _____

**8.** guardrail _____ _____

**9.** headquarters _____ _____

**10.** earthquake _____ _____

**Directions:** Read each sentence aloud and circle the words that have softening consonants or oddball consonants. This would be a great time to have your study buddy dictate the sentences to you.

**11.** Cross the bridge to the queen's palace.

**12.** Squeeze lemon extract into the cake mix.

**13.** Your voice is unclear on that cell phone.

**14.** Recite the magic words and the gypsy will appear.

**15.** Connect the cables to the microprocessor.

**16.** Quench your thirst at the refreshment center.

**17.** Does your fax machine have a digital quartz display?

**18.** Export the quartz stones from the quarry to Germany.

**19.** Meet the general at the army headquarters.

**20.** Cover the angel hair pasta with cellophane.

**My score for Exercise 6 is _____ out of 20.**

# ANSWERS

## Exercise 1

1. quilt
2. quip
3. quality
4. equality
5. sequins
6. sticky
7. except
8. exult
9. expose
10. exact

## Exercise 3

1. exit
2. exact
3. exile
4. exist
5. exit
6. quit
7. quail
8. queen
9. quaint
10. quiver
11. squeaky
12. squirt
13. squint
14. squeeze
15. squeal
16. six
17. wax
18. fox
19. tax
20. fax

## Exercise 4

1. quit
2. quill
3. qualify
4. equipment
5. sequels
6. sixty
7. excerpt
8. exact
9. explore
10. extract

## Exercise 5

1. extract
2. quit
3. quill
4. explore
5. qualify
6. exact
7. equipment
8. excerpt
9. sequels
10. sixty

## Exercise 6

1. gentle      man
2. express     way
3. tax         payer
4. bridge      work
5. face        lift
6. pace        maker
7. police      man
8. guard       rail
9. head        quarters
10. earth      quake

11. bridge, queen's, palace
12. Squeeze, extract, mix
13. voice, cell
14. Recite, magic, gypsy
15. microprocessor

16. Quench, center
17. fax, digital, quartz
18. Export, quartz, quarry, Germany
19. general, headquarters
20. angel, cellophane

# LESSON 12

# SILENCE!

So far, the lessons in this book have taught spelling skills by emphasizing letter/sound relationships. This lesson, however, focuses on letters that make no sound. These are some of the most difficult letters to remember. Although they may be absolutely silent, you still have to write them if you want people to know what you mean.

## EXERCISE 1: EYEBALLING SPELLING LIST 12

**Directions:** Sweep your eyes across the line from left to right and back again. Do it quickly. Circle the word in each line that looks different from the others on that line.

Are you ready? Get set . . . Go!

| | | | |
|---|---|---|---|
| **1.** writer | writer | writer | writes |
| **2.** wrist | wrist | wrist | writ |
| **3.** wrestling | whistling | wrestling | wrestling |
| **4.** rhymes | rhythms | rhythms | rhythms |
| **5.** rhinoceros | rhinoceros | rhombus | rhinoceros |
| **6.** rhinestone | rhinoceros | rhinestone | rhinestone |
| **7.** knowledge | knowledge | acknowledge | knowledge |

| **8.** knit | knit | knit | knife |
|---|---|---|---|
| **9.** gnats | gnaws | gnaws | gnaws |
| **10.** resign | design | design | design |

Check your answers with the answer key at the end of this lesson.
**My score for Exercise 1 is _____ out of 10.**

## REFLECTION

Go back to the words that are the same on each line in Exercise 1. Locate the letters *wr*, *rh*, *kn*, and *gn*. These letters are partners. When they're together, only one is allowed to speak. In other words, only one out of the two letters represents a sound. How will you know which letter represents a sound? You can find out by doing Exercise 2, Sound Inventory.

## EXERCISE 2: SOUND INVENTORY

**Directions:** Listen to yourself as you read each group of words aloud. **You must read the words out loud.** The letters and sounds in each group have something in common. Put a circle around the letters that are the same in each group and then write them on the lines provided.

| **Group 1** | **Group 2** |
|---|---|
| wrap | rhyme |
| wreath | Rhine (river) |
| wren | rhumba |
| _____ | _____ |

| **Group 3** | **Group 4** | |
|---|---|---|
| knit | gnat | sign |
| know | gnaw | resign |
| knot | gnarl | design |
| _____ | _____ | |

In Group 1, the common letters are *wr*. Can you hear the sound of the letters *wr*? Which letter is silent? If you need help, use slash marks to break the words into sounds. The word *wrap* should be written as /r/ă/p/, and the word *writer* should be written as /r/ī/t/e/r/. Now can you hear the sound? The letter *w* is silent, and the letter *r* has the sound found in the clue word *radio*.

In Group 2, the common letters are *rh*. Can you hear the sound of the letters *rh*? Which letter is silent? If you need help, use slash marks to break the words into sounds. The word *rhyme* should be written as /r/ī/m/ and the word *Rhine* should be written as /r/ī/n/. Now can you hear the sound? The letter *h* is silent, and the letter *r* has the sound found in the clue word **radio**.

In Group 3, the common letters are *kn*. Can you hear the sound of the letters *kn*? Which letter is silent? If you need help, use slash marks to break the words into sounds. The word *knot* should be written as /n/ŏ/t/ and the word *knit* should be written as /n/ĭ/t/. Now can you hear the sound? The letter *k* is silent and the letter *n* has the sound found in the clue word **needle**.

In Group 4, the common letters are *gn*. Can you hear the sound of the letters *gn*? Which letter is silent? If you need help, use slash marks to break the words into sounds. The word *gnat* should be written as /n/ă/t/ and the word *sign* should be written /s/ī/n/. Now can you hear the sound? The letter *g* is silent and the letter *n* has the sound found in the clue word **needle**.

## REFLECTION

What consonants did you learn about in this lesson? _____

What sound do *kn* and *gn* represent? _____

What sound do *wr* and *rh* represent? _____

Where are these silent letters located in the words? _____

The sound of the letter *n*, as found in the clue word **needle**, is represented by the letters *kn* and *gn*. The sound of the letter *r*, as found in the clue word **radio**, is represented by the letters *wr* and *rh*. Most of the time, silent letters are located at the beginning of a word. The letters *gn*, though, can be located both at the beginning and at the end of a word. For practice with these silent letters, move on to Exercise 3.

## EXERCISE 3: PRACTICE WITH SUBSTITUTION

**Directions:** Remove the first consonant and substitute it with the letters *kn*, *gn*, *wr*, or *rh*.

**1.** neck _____     **6.** list _____

**2.** rack _____     **7.** cob _____

**3.** bats _____     **8.** buckle _____

**4.** raw _____     **9.** low _____

**5.** line _____     **10.** lock _____

Check your answers with the answer key at the end of this lesson.

**My score for Exercise 3 is _____ out of 10.**

## EXERCISE 4: PRACTICE WRITING SPELLING LIST 12

**Directions:** Go back to Exercise 1. Look at the three words that are the same on each line. Write each of these words only once on the lines below. This would be a good time to have your study buddy dictate the words to you.

1. _____      6. _____
2. _____      7. _____
3. _____      8. _____
4. _____      9. _____
5. _____      10. _____

Consult your dictionary if the meaning of a word is unfamiliar to you.

Check your answers with the answer key at the end of this lesson.

**My score for Exercise 4 is _____ out of 10.**

## EXERCISE 5: PRACTICE WRITING SPELLING LIST 12 IN CONTEXT

**Directions:** Use the words from Exercise 4 to complete the following phrases. For added practice, rewrite the entire phrase in your own sentence on the line provided.

**1.** a gerbil _____

_____

**2.** _____ a sweater

_____

**3.** a published _____

_____

**4.** a watch on my left _____

_____

**5.** a _____ match

_____

**6.** listen for the _____

_____

**7.** _____ a wedding dress

_____

**8.** a _____ necklace

_____

**9.** a book of _____

_____

**10.** the endangered _____

_____

Check your answers with the answer key at the end of this lesson. Only the words that go in the blanks are given, since everyone will create different sentences. **My score for Exercise 5 is _____ out of 10.**

Do you want more challenging words with the combinations *kn, gn, wr,* and *rh*? Try these! Call on your study buddy to dictate them to you as you write them in your notebook. Consult your dictionary if you need to so that you can use the words correctly.

| | | |
|---|---|---|
| **kn**uckle | **kn**ighthood | ac**kn**owledgment |
| **wr**apper | **wr**inkle | **wr**istband |
| **rh**eumatism | **rh**etorical | **rh**ombus |
| beni**gn** | campai**gn** | |

## EXERCISE 6: WHAT HAVE YOU LEARNED?

**Directions:** Read each compound word aloud. Then rewrite each compound word on the lines provided as two separate words.

**1.** wrongdoer _____ _____
**2.** wristband _____ _____
**3.** doorknob _____ _____
**4.** knockout _____ _____
**5.** knapsack _____ _____
**6.** shipwreck _____ _____
**7.** kneepads _____ _____
**8.** signpost _____ _____
**9.** signboard _____ _____
**10.** kneecap _____ _____

**Directions:** Read each phrase aloud and circle the words that have the silent letters you learned in this lesson.

11. my favorite writer
12. real estate signs on the lawn
13. the queen reigns
14. the foreign invaders
15. a gnarled tree

16. a knight in shining armor
17. a rhyming word
18. wrapping presents
19. design women's clothing
20. knit a sweater

Check your answers with the answer key at the end of this lesson.
**My score for Exercise 6 is _____ out of 20.**

## ANSWERS

### Exercise 1
1. writes
2. writ
3. whistling
4. rhymes
5. rhombus
6. rhinoceros
7. acknowledge
8. knife
9. gnats
10. resign

### Exercise 4
1. writer
2. wrist
3. wrestling
4. rhythms
5. rhinoceros
6. rhinestone
7. knowledge
8. knit
9. gnaws
10. design

### Exercise 3
1. wreck
2. knack
3. gnats
4. gnaw
5. Rhine
6. wrist
7. knob
8. knuckle
9. know
10. knock

### Exercise 5
1. gnaws
2. knit
3. writer
4. wrist
5. wrestling
6. rhythm
7. design
8. rhinestone
9. knowledge
10. rhinoceros

## Exercise 6

| | | | |
|---|---|---|---|
| **1.** wrong | doer | **11.** writer | |
| **2.** wrist | band | **12.** signs | |
| **3.** door | knob | **13.** reigns | |
| **4.** knock | out | **14.** foreign | |
| **5.** knap | sack | **15.** gnarled | |
| **6.** ship | wreck | **16.** knight | |
| **7.** knee | pads | **17.** rhyming | |
| **8.** sign | post | **18.** wrapping | |
| **9.** sign | board | **19.** design | |
| **10.** knee | cap | **20.** knit | |

# LESSON

# 13

# SILENT LETTERS AND DOUBLE TROUBLE

There are more silent letters in this lesson. Some of them have two letters that are exactly the same, and so are known as **double consonants**. Look carefully to see *where* these silent double consonants appear in a word.

### EXERCISE 1: EYEBALLING SPELLING LIST 13

**Directions:** Sweep your eyes across the line from left to right and back again. Do it quickly. Circle the word in each line that looks different from the others on that line.

Are you ready? Get set . . . Go!

| | | | |
|---|---|---|---|
| **1.** crams | crumbs | crumbs | crumbs |
| **2.** thumb | thumb | thumb | hum |
| **3.** limbs | limps | limbs | limbs |
| **4.** spell | spell | shell | spell |
| **5.** mess | mess | mess | mist |
| **6.** drills | dwells | dwells | dwells |
| **7.** winker | wicker | wicker | wicker |

| | | | |
|---|---|---|---|
| **8.** pocket | pocket | pocket | picket |
| **9.** cracker | cracker | canker | cracker |
| **10.** staff | staff | staff | stiff |

Check your answers with the answer key at the end of this lesson.
**My score for Exercise 1 is _____ out of 10.**

## REFLECTION

Go back to the words that are the same on each line in Exercise 1. Locate the letters *mb*, *ck*, *ll*, *ss*, and *ff*. These letters are partners. When they're together, only one is allowed to speak. In other words, only one out of the two letters represents a sound. You can probably guess the sound of the double letters *ff*, *ll*, and *ss*, but what sound do the letters *mb* and *ck* represent? You can find out by doing Exercise 2, Sound Inventory.

## EXERCISE 2: SOUND INVENTORY

**Directions:** Listen to yourself as you read each group of words aloud. **You must read the words out loud.** The letters and sounds in each group have something in common. Put a circle around the letters that are the same in each group and then write the two letters on the lines provided.

**Group 1**

| bless | stiff | drill |
|---|---|---|
| mess | cliff | gull |
| dress | cuff | swell |
| ____ | ____ | ____ |

**Group 2**

comb
tomb
limb

____

**Group 3**

rock
trick
deck

____

In Group 1, the common letters are *ss*, *ff*, and *ll*. Can you hear the sound of the letters *ss*, *ff*, and *ll*? Which letters are silent? If you need help, use slash marks to break the words into sounds. The word *bless* should be written as /b/l/ ĕ /s/, the word *staff* should be written as /s/t/ ă /f/, and the word *drill* should be written as /d/r/ ĭ /l/. Now can you hear the sounds? Only one of the double letters makes a sound. The letters *s*, *f*, and *l* represent the sounds as found in the clue words *sun*, *fork*, and *lemon*.

In Group 2, the common letters are *mb*. Can you hear the sound of the letters *mb*? Which letter is silent? If you need help, use slash marks to break the words into sounds using the letter/sound strategy. The word *comb* should be written as /c/ō/m/ and the word *limb* should be written as /l/ĭ/m/. Now can you hear the sound? The letter *b* is silent, and the letter *m* represents the sound as found in the clue word *mailbox*.

In Group 3, the common letters are *ck*. Can you hear the sound of the letters *ck*? Which letter is silent? If you need help, use slash marks to break the words into sounds. The word *rock* should be written as /r/ ŏ /k/ and the word *trick* should be written as /t/r/ĭ/k/. Now can you hear the sound? The letter *c* is silent and the letter *k* represents the sound as found in the clue word *key*.

## REFLECTION

What consonants did you learn about in this lesson? _____

What sounds do the letters *mb* and *ck* represent? _____

What sounds do the letters *ll* and *ff* and *ss* represent? _____

What can you say about the location of all these double or silent consonants?

_____

_____

The sound /m/, as found in the clue word *mailbox*, is represented by the letters *mb*. The sound /k/, as found in the clue word *key*, is represented by the letters *ck*.

The double letters only make one sound. This means that *ll* sounds like one letter, *l*, as found in the clue word *lemon*; *ss* is like the letter *s*, as found in the clue word *sun*; and *ff* is like the letter *f*, as found in the clue word *fork*. All of these consonants—double or silent—are located at the end of a word.

## EXERCISE 3: PRACTICE SUBSTITUTING WITH ENDING CONSONANTS

**Directions:** Change the final consonant in each word to *mb*, *ck*, *ss*, *ll*, or *ff*. A few have been done for you. For some words, there is more than one answer.

**1.** top    *tomb*    _____    _____

**2.** dug    _____    _____    _____

**3.** nut    *null*    _____

**4.** lap    _____    _____    _____

**5.** gum    _____

**6.** plug _____  _____

**7.** let _____

**8.** mix _____  _____

**9.** pat _____  _____

**10.** pup ___*puss*___  _____  _____  _____

Check your answers with the answer key at the end of this lesson.

**My score for Exercise 3 is _____ out of 10.**

## EXERCISE 4: PRACTICE WRITING SPELLING LIST 13

**Directions:** Go back to Exercise 1. Look at the three words that are the same on each line. Write each of these words only once on the lines below. This would be a good time to have your study buddy dictate the words to you.

**1.** _____    **6.** _____

**2.** _____    **7.** _____

**3.** _____    **8.** _____

**4.** _____    **9.** _____

**5.** _____    **10.** _____

Consult your dictionary if the meaning of a word is unfamiliar to you.

Check your answers with the answer key at the end of this lesson.

**My score for Exercise 4 is _____ out of 10.**

## EXERCISE 5: PRACTICE WRITING SPELLING LIST 13 IN CONTEXT

**Directions:** Use the words from Exercise 4 to complete the following phrases. For added practice, rewrite the entire phrase in your own sentence on the provided line.

**1.** cheese on a _____

_____

**2.** a _____ basket

_____

**3.** _____ in a cave

_____

**4.** _____ on a tablecloth

_____

**5.** a green _____

_____

**6.** the _____ of a tree

_____

**7.** _____ the words correctly

_____

**8.** a wallet in my _____

_____

**9.** clean up the _____

_____

**10.** dependable _____

_____

Check your answers with the answer key at the end of this lesson. Only the words that go in the blanks are given, since everyone will create different sentences. **My score for Exercise 5 is _____ out of 10.**

## VARIATIONS

All of the following words contain silent letters, either vowels or consonants. The fact that these letters are silent doesn't mean they don't affect the sound of a word. For instance, without the *u* in *biscuit*, you'd have *biscit*, which, according to the soft *c* rule, would be pronounced /b/ĭ/s/ĭ/t/. The *t* in *listen* gives a different sound than would be heard in *lisen*, which would have a long /ī/ sound. This is why it is said that these silent letters "hold a place."

Read all the following words aloud. Look at the bold letters in each word as you say the word. Have your study buddy dictate the words to you while you write them in your notebook.

| | | | |
|---|---|---|---|
| build | listen | si**gh** | **gu**ess |
| bis**c**uit | fasten | high | **gu**ide |
| moisten | thou**gh** | **gu**itar | |
| sketch | dau**gh**ter | | |

Do you want more challenging words that contain the *mb*, *ck*, *ss*, *ll*, or *ff* combinations? Try these! Call on your study buddy to dictate them to you as you write them in your notebook. Consult your dictionary if you need to so that you can use the words correctly.

| classmate | passkey | **gu**ardianship |
| passbook | password | dis**gu**ise |
| grasshopper | **gu**idance | |

## EXERCISE 6: WHAT HAVE YOU LEARNED?

In Lessons 12 and 13, you learned how silent letters represent no sound but still "hold a place." These silent letters pose a problem when using the letter/sound relationship strategy. Therefore, your memory is your guide. If you have done all the practice exercises diligently, you will have a good chance of spelling the words correctly. This last exercise offers you even more practice. Call upon your study buddy and get to work!

**Directions:** Read each sentence aloud. Circle all the words that have silent letters you learned in Lessons 12 and 13.

1. Listen to the sighs of complaint from that naughty child.
2. The wicker basket will hold wine, cheese, and crackers.
3. The tour guides will present a valid parking sticker to the guard.
4. The plumber will repair the gushing water pipe with a wrench.
5. Moisten the soil and plant the hollyhock seeds.
6. Five new employees have joined the staff at Mill Pass Bank.
7. Use a drill to spell the name on the tombstone.
8. The seagulls dwell by the seashore.
9. The messy table was filled with crumbs from the rhubarb pie.
10. Do you know whether the tree's limbs were destroyed by the lightning storm?

**Directions:** Read each compound word aloud. Then rewrite each compound word as two separate words. These words are loaded with silent letters; see if you can find them all.

11. bombshell _____ _____
12. guardrail _____ _____
13. sketchbook _____ _____
14. guesswork _____ _____
15. highway _____ _____
16. switchblade _____ _____
17. guidebook _____ _____

**18.** witchcraft _____ _____
**19.** thighbone _____ _____
**20.** crackerjack _____ _____

Check your answers with the answer key at the end of this lesson.
**My score for Exercise 6 is \_\_\_\_\_ out of 20.**

## ANSWERS

### Exercise 1

**1.** crams
**2.** hum
**3.** limps
**4.** shell
**5.** mist
**6.** drills
**7.** winker
**8.** picket
**9.** canker
**10.** stiff

### Exercise 3

**1.** tomb, toll, toss
**2.** duck, dull, dumb
**3.** null, numb
**4.** lass, lack, lamb
**5.** gull
**6.** pluck, plumb
**7.** less
**8.** mill, miss
**9.** pack, pass
**10.** puss, pull, puck, puff

### Exercise 4

**1.** crumbs
**2.** thumb
**3.** limbs
**4.** spell
**5.** mess
**6.** dwells
**7.** wicker
**8.** pocket
**9.** cracker
**10.** staff

### Exercise 5

**1.** cracker
**2.** wicker
**3.** dwells
**4.** crumbs
**5.** thumb
**6.** limbs
**7.** spell
**8.** pocket
**9.** mess
**10.** staff

## Exercise 6

1. Listen, sighs, naughty
2. wicker, crackers
3. guides, sticker, guard
4. plumber, wrench
5. Moisten, hollyhock
6. staff, Mill, Pass
7. drill, spell, tombstone
8. seagulls, dwell
9. messy, filled, crumbs, rhubarb
10. know, limbs, lightning

11. bomb      shell
12. guard     rail
13. sketch    book
14. guess     work
15. high      way
16. switch    blade
17. guide     book
18. witch     craft
19. thigh     bone
20. cracker   jack

# LESSON 14

# EXPAND . . . EXPANSION

You have read the phrase *expand your pool of spelling words* many times in this book. This lesson in particular will help you do this. Take a look at the title. Going from *Expand* to *Expansion* is only a matter of adding a simple ending—*sion*. Once you learn the letter/sound relationship for this ending, learning any number of advanced spelling words will be very simple.

## EXERCISE 1: EYEBALLING SPELLING LIST 14

**Directions:** Sweep your eyes across the line from left to right and back again. Do it quickly. Circle the word in each line that looks different from the others on that line.

Are you ready? Get set . . . Go!

| | | | |
|---|---|---|---|
| **1.** detection | decision | decision | decision |
| **2.** depletion | depletion | deletion | depletion |
| **3.** simplification | simplification | simplification | verification |
| **4.** condition | composition | composition | composition |
| **5.** inspection | inspection | inspection | inflection |
| **6.** evolution | evolution | elocution | evolution |
| **7.** invitation | invitation | invitation | imitation |

| | | | |
|---|---|---|---|
| **8.** vacation | vacation | vaccination | vacation |
| **9.** erosion | erosion | erosion | election |
| **10.** nation | nation | nation | notion |

Check your answers with the answer key at the end of this lesson.
**My score for Exercise 1 is _____ out of 10.**

## REFLECTION

Go back to the words that are the same in each line. Look for the letter *i* near the end of each word. What letters precede (go before) the letter *i*?

_____

The letter *i* is preceded by the letters *t* and *s*. Look for the letters *ti* and *si* in each word; then move on to Exercise 2, Sound Inventory, to hear the sounds these letters represent.

## EXERCISE 2: SOUND INVENTORY

**Directions:** Listen to yourself as you read each group of words aloud. **You must read the words out loud.** The letters and sounds in each group have something in common. Put a circle around the letters that are the same in each group and then write them on the lines provided.

| **Group 1** | **Group 2** |
|---|---|
| mansion | action |
| pension | nation |
| expansion | motion |
| _____ | _____ |

In Group 1, the common letters are *sion*. Can you hear the sound of the letters *sion*? If not, use slash marks to break the words into sounds. The word *mansion* is represented by the sounds /m/ă/n/sh/ŭ/n/. The letters *si* sound like /sh/, as found in the clue word **shake**. Now can you hear the sound? The letters *sion* represent the sound /sh/ŭ/n/.

In Group 2, the common letters are *tion*. Can you hear the sound of the letters *tion*? If not, use slash marks to break the words into sounds. The word *nation* is represented by the sounds /n/ā/sh/ŭ/n/. The letters *ti* sound like /sh/, as found in the clue word **shake**. Now can you hear the sound? The letters *tion* represent the sound /sh/ŭ/n/.

# REFLECTION

What letters represent the sound of /sh/? _____

What sounds do the letters sion and *tion* represent? _____

The English language chooses to use the letters *si* and *ti* to represent the sound of /sh/. The letters *tion* and *sion* represent the ending that sounds like *shun*.

Move on to Exercise 3 to practice spelling words with the endings *tion* and *sion*.

# EXERCISE 3: THE EXPANSION OF WORDS

**Directions:** Each of the following words is written as it sounds. Write each word with its correct spelling. The /sh/ sound is represented by the letters *ti*. The first word has been done for you.

1. /p/ŏ/p/ū/l/ā/sh/ŭ/n/      *population*
2. / ě /d/ū/c/ā/sh/ŭ/n/      _____
3. /c/ŏ/m/ū/n/ĭ/c/ā/sh/ŭ/n/      _____
4. /l/ō/c/ā/sh/ŭ/n/      _____
5. /ĭ/m/ĭ/t/ā/sh/ŭ/n/      _____
6. /c/ŏ/m/p/l/ē/sh/ŭ/n/      _____
7. / ĕ /k/s/p/ĭr/ā/sh/ŭ/n/      _____
8. /ĭ/n/v/ě/n/sh/ŭ/n/      _____
9. /ä/d/ŏ /p/sh/ŭ/n/      _____
10. /ĭ/n/v/ě/s/t/ĭ/g/ā/sh/ŭ/n/      _____
11. / ě /k/s/p/or/t/ā/sh/ŭ/n/      _____
12. /d/ē/p/or/t/ā/sh/ŭ/n/      _____
13. /v/ĭ/s/ĭ /t/ā/sh/ŭ/n/      _____
14. /ŏ/b/s/er/v/ā/sh/ŭ/n/      _____
15. / ě /k/s/p/l/ă/n/ā/sh/ŭ/n/      _____
16. /ĭ/n/s/t/ĭ/t/ū/sh/ŭ/n/      _____
17. /t/ ă/k/s/ā/sh/ŭ/n/      _____
18. /ĭ/n/s/er/sh/ŭ/n/      _____
19. /au/t/ō/m/ā/sh/ŭ/n/      _____
20. /ē/kw/ā/sh/ŭ/n/      _____

**Directions:** Each of the following words is written as it sounds. Write each word with the correct spelling. The /sh/ sound is represented by the letters *si*.

21. /s/ŭ/s/p/ě/n/sh/ŭ/n/      _____
22. / ě /k/s/p/ă/n/sh/ŭ/n/      _____

**23.** /m/ă/n/sh/ŭ/n/ _____

**24.** /l/ē/sh/ŭ/n/ _____

Check your answers with the answer key at the end of this lesson.
**My score for Exercise 3 is _____ out of 24.**

## EXERCISE 4: PRACTICE WRITING SPELLING LIST 14

**Directions:** Go back to Exercise 1. Look at the three words that are the same on each line. Write each of these words only once on the lines below. This would be a good time to have your study buddy dictate the words to you.

**1.** _____    **6.** _____

**2.** _____    **7.** _____

**3.** _____    **8.** _____

**4.** _____    **9.** _____

**5.** _____    **10.** _____

Consult your dictionary if the meaning of a word is unfamiliar to you.

Check your answers with the answer key at the end of this lesson.

**My score for Exercise 4 is _____ out of 10.**

## EXERCISE 5: PRACTICE WRITING SPELLING LIST 14 IN CONTEXT

**1.** a wedding _____

_____

**2.** a two-week _____

_____

**3.** soil _____

_____

**4.** a jury's _____

_____

**5.** _____ of oil and gasoline

_____

**6.** your car's _____ sticker

_____

**7.** a _____ of the facts

_____

**8.** humanity's _____ through time

_____

**9.** a 500-word _____

_____

**10.** a united _____

_____

Check your answers with the answer key at the end of this lesson. Only the words that go in the blanks are given, since everyone will create different sentences. **My score for Exercise 5 is _____ out of 10.**

## VARIATIONS

Some words double the letter *s*. In those words, the sound of /sh/ŭ/n/ is represented by the letters *ssion*. Below are some examples.

| | | | |
|---|---|---|---|
| mis**sion** | omis**sion** | emis**sion** | permis**sion** |
| commis**sion** | admis**sion** | transmis**sion** | depres**sion** |
| expres**sion** | impres**sion** | compres**sion** | concus**sion** |
| percus**sion** | discus**sion** | ses**sion** | pas**sion** |

The following words also have the letters *si*, but these letters represent the combined sound of /z/ and /h/, as found in the Consonant Key. In these words, the *si* makes a sort of vibrating sound. You can hear it clearly in the word *television* and words like these.

| | | | |
|---|---|---|---|
| vi**si**on | provi**si**on | supervi**si**on | fu**si**on |
| confu**si**on | transfu**si**on | illu**si**on | conclu**si**on |
| preci**si**on | ero**si**on | | |

Do you want more challenging words with the /sh/ŭ/n/ sound? Try these! Call on your study buddy to dictate them to you as you write them in your notebook.

| | | | |
|---|---|---|---|
| classifica**tion** | participa**tion** | equaliza**tion** | nationaliza**tion** |
| affirma**tion** | defama**tion** | institu**tion** | mummifica**tion** |
| constitu**tion** | restitu**tion** | rendi**tion** | organiza**tion** |
| ora**tion** | | | |

## EXERCISE 6: WHAT HAVE YOU LEARNED?

**Directions:** Select one word in parentheses to complete each sentence correctly.

1. The financial _____ offers instant cash access.
   (institute, institution)
2. The pamphlet will provide an _____ of the health benefits.
   (explain, explanation)
3. The salesperson will receive a two-week _____.
   (vacate, vacation)
4. Did you receive the order _____ by e-mail?
   (confirmation, confirm)
5. There is no _____ from the customer-service link.
   (communicate, communication)
6. The credit card will offer retail _____ service.
   (protect, protection)
7. _____ of the computer will be done by an authorized dealer.
   (Install, Installation)
8. The _____ date is stamped on every bottle of soda.
   (expire, expiration)
9. The claims will be processed after the _____.
   (invest, investigation)
10. Mail _____ is a service provided by the U.S. Post Office.
    (collect, collection)

Check your answers with the answer key at the end of this lesson.

**My score for Exercise 6 is _____ out of 10.**

Once you've finished filling in the blanks, read each sentence aloud. Call on your study buddy to dictate the sentences to you. They're challenging, but you can do it!

## ANSWERS

### Exercise 1

1. detection
2. deletion
3. verification
4. condition
5. inflection
6. elocution
7. imitation
8. vaccination
9. election
10. notion

## Exercise 3

1. population
2. education
3. communication
4. location
5. imitation
6. completion
7. expiration
8. invention
9. adoption
10. investigation
11. exportation
12. deportation
13. visitation
14. observation
15. explanation
16. institution
17. taxation
18. insertion
19. automation
20. equation
21. suspension
22. expansion
23. mansion
24. lesion

## Exercise 4

1. decision
2. depletion
3. simplification
4. composition

5. inspection
6. evolution
7. invitation
8. vacation
9. erosion
10. nation

## Exercise 5

1. invitation
2. vacation
3. erosion
4. decision
5. depletion
6. inspection
7. simplification
8. evolution
9. composition
10. nation

## Exercise 6

1. institution
2. explanation
3. vacation
4. confirmation
5. communication
6. protection
7. Installation
8. expiration
9. investigation
10. collection

# LESSON

# 15

# BEAT THE STRESS

This lesson is about the rhythm of words. Rhythm is the musical quality of words caused by the "beats" you hear in a word and how these beats are stressed or accented. These beats are called **syllables**. Spelling will be easier when you learn to write words beat by beat or syllable by syllable. Doesn't that sound rhythmical?

## EXERCISE 1: EYEBALLING SPELLING LIST 15

**Directions:** Sweep your eyes across the line from left to right and back again. Do it quickly. Circle the word in each line that looks different from the others on that line.

Are you ready? Get set . . . Go!

| | | | |
|---|---|---|---|
| **1.** sparkles | sparklers | sparklers | sparklers |
| **2.** slippery | sloppy | slippery | slippery |
| **3.** labeling | labeling | label | labeling |
| **4.** mysteries | mysteries | mysteries | mystery |
| **5.** music | musical | musical | musical |
| **6.** desert | deserting | deserting | deserting |
| **7.** pretty | pretty | pretty | prettier |

| | | | |
|---|---|---|---|
| **8.** billowing | billowed | billowing | billowing |
| **9.** skinnier | skinnier | skinnier | skinny |
| **10.** projected | projected | project | projected |

Check your answers with the answer key at the end of this lesson.
**My score for Exercise 1 is \_\_\_\_\_ out of 10.**

## REFLECTION

Go back to the words that are different on each line. Compare them to the three identical words. What sets the odd words apart in rows 1–10?

_____

What endings do you see? _____

_____

The words are almost the same on each line, except for the endings. You should have found *ed*, *ier*, *ing*, *y*, *al*, *ies*, and *ers*. These are all endings that give the main word an added beat or two. They are **syllables**. A syllable can be either a consonant and a vowel or a vowel alone. Move on to Exercise 2, Sound Inventory, to hear fully the beats or syllables in a word.

## EXERCISE 2: SOUND INVENTORY

**Directions:** Follow the arrows from left to right as you read the following lines of words. Read each line aloud or have your study buddy read them to you. This time, listen for the number of beats or syllables in each word and write the number of beats you hear on the provided space. For example, the word *hum* has one syllable. The word *hummer* has two syllables. *Hummingbird* has three syllables. You try it.

| | | | | | |
|---|---|---|---|---|---|
| **1.** ham | _1_ | hammer | _2_ | hammering | _3_ |
| **2.** slip | _1_ | slipper | \_\_\_\_ | slippery | \_\_\_\_ |
| **3.** rob | \_\_\_\_ | robber | \_\_\_\_ | robberies | \_\_\_\_ |
| **4.** visit | \_\_\_\_ | visited | \_\_\_\_ | visitation | \_\_\_\_ |
| **5.** limit | \_\_\_\_ | limited | \_\_\_\_ | limitation | \_\_\_\_ |

Check your answers with the answer key at the end of this lesson.
**My score for Exercise 2 is \_\_\_\_\_ out of 15 (three answers on a line).**

For numbers 1–3, the first word in the line had one syllable, the next word across had two syllables, and the final word on the line had three syllables. Do you see that every syllable has a vowel? Separate the syllables in your mind as you say the word aloud before you try to spell any word on paper. You have just acquired another spelling strategy—spelling the words syllable by syllable.

Move on to the next part of Sound Inventory to identify the first vowel in each syllable.

**Directions:** Read each of the following groups of words aloud. Listen very carefully to the vowel (the second sound) in the first syllable. Which group has the short vowel and which group has the long vowel sound in the first syllable? Write the word *long* or *short* on the line below the group.

If you need help recalling the sounds of the vowels, refer to the Letter/Sound Relationship Key in the introduction.

| Group 1 | | Group 2 | |
|---------|------|---------|------|
| lim | it | mi | ser |
| ped | al | tu | lip |
| sav | age | la | bel |
| mod | el | de | mon |
| pun | ish | clo | ver |

Group 1 has a short vowel in the first syllable. When a vowel sits between two consonants, the sound is usually short. This also can be called a **closed syllable**.

Group 2 has a long vowel in the first syllable. When a vowel ends the syllable, the sound is usually long. This also can be called an **open syllable**.

## EXERCISE 3: SOUND AND MEANING

You need to know the following general rule about vowels in open and closed syllables, because changing the stress, or accent, in a word can change a syllable from open to closed or vice versa. This change leads to a change in the sound—and meaning—of a word.

Look at these two words:

mi nute´    min´ ute

They are spelled exactly the same but are written with spaces between them to denote syllables. The first word has an **open syllable** and the other has a **closed syllable**. Thus, the first vowel sound is different in each word.

Some syllables are emphasized more than others in a word. This is called **stress**. Stress can bounce from syllable to syllable. The dictionary uses an accent mark (′) to show which syllable is stressed or emphasized when spoken aloud. The vowel in a stressed syllable can either be long or short.

Say the following two words aloud:

mi nute′      min′ ute

In the first word, the first syllable has a long vowel /ī/ and the second syllable is stressed. In the second word, the first syllable has a short vowel /ĭ/ and the first syllable is stressed. Read the following sentences to help you pronounce the two words correctly.

The detective asked the witness for even the minute (mi nute′) details of the robbery.
The fax will be sent in a minute (min′ ute) or two.

You should have figured out by now that changing the stress also can change the meaning of a word. There are many words like this, and the letter/sound relationship strategy holds true for all of them. If you write what you hear, you will have no problem.

**Directions:** Practice hearing the stress by reading the following words. You will see that the stress bounces from the first to the second syllable as you move down the list. Read the pairs of words and write whether the first vowel is long or short. Read the sentences aloud to help you.

| WORD | VOWEL |
|---|---|
| **1.** re fuse′ | long /ē/ |
| The automated teller machine refused to accept the debit card. | |
| **2.** ref′ use | short /ĕ/ |
| Financial institutions are inundated with paper. Who will cart the refuse away? | |
| **3.** min′ ute | _____ |
| The laser printer prints 50 pages each minute and 100 pages in two minutes. | |
| **4.** mi nute′ | _____ |
| The shredder cut the paper into minute pieces. | |
| **5.** rec′ ord | _____ |
| The paper receipt is a record of the sales transaction. | |

**6.** re cord´          _____

A camcorder will record your memories on tape.

**7.** proj´ ect          _____

Online customer service is a project for this new company.

**8.** pro ject´          _____

What do you project will be the expandability of this computer system?

Check your answers with the answer key at the end of this lesson.

**My score for Exercise 3 is _____ out of 8.**

# REFLECTION

What is the musical quality in a word called? _____

What are the beats in a word called? _____

How will the syllables strategy help the speller? _____

_____

What can you say about the vowel sound in a closed syllable?

_____

What can you say about the vowel sound in an open syllable?

_____

What happens if the stress changes in a word? _____

_____

The musical quality of a word is called **rhythm**. The beats you hear are called **syllables**. Spelling can be made easier by writing what you hear, syllable by syllable. The vowel in an open syllable, like the syllable *mi* in the word *mi nute'*, is usually a long sound. The vowel in a closed syllable, like the syllable *min* in the word *min' ute*, is usually a short sound. A syllable can be emphasized or stressed. When the stress changes in the same word, it also changes its meaning.

By now, you should be very comfortable with the letter/sound relationship strategy and be quite aware that there are exceptions to this strategy. This holds true for the vowels. A vowel can lose its long or short sound to something called a **schwa**. This happens in multisyllabic words and is represented by an upside-down letter *e*. When a vowel sounds like the vowel in the word *of*, that vowel is said to have a schwa sound. Any vowel, *a, e, i, o, u*, or *y*, can lose its original sound to a schwa. The following are a few words that have the vowel as a schwa sound. The bold vowel is the schwa.

| | | | |
|---|---|---|---|
| doctor | comatose | ign**o**ramus | infantile |
| cha**u**vinism | lucrative | mediocr**e** | neighb**o**r |

Any vowel can be represented by the schwa sound, so at times the letter/sound relationship can be difficult. The schwa sound will appear again in the following lessons.

## EXERCISE 4: PRACTICE WRITING SPELLING LIST 15

**Directions:** Go back to Exercise 1. Look at the three words that are the same on each line. Write each of these words only once on the lines below. This would be a good time to have your study buddy dictate the words to you.

1. _____          6. _____
2. _____          7. _____
3. _____          8. _____
4. _____          9. _____
5. _____          10. _____

Consult your dictionary if the meaning of a word is unfamiliar to you.

Check your answers with the answer key at the end of this lesson.

**My score for Exercise 4 is _____ out of 10.**

## EXERCISE 5: PRACTICE WRITING SPELLING LIST 15 IN CONTEXT

**Directions:** Use the words from Exercise 4 to complete the following phrases. For added practice, rewrite the entire phrase in your own sentence on the provided line.

**1.** a _____, waxed floor

_____

**2.** a _____ play on Broadway

_____

**3.** unsolved _____

**4.** _____ the army

_____

**5.** _____ clouds of smoke

_____

**6.** _____ sales for next month

_____

**7.** _____ the food products

_____

**8.** _____ flowers

_____

**9.** _____ after a diet

_____

**10.** _____ for the Fourth of July

_____

Check your answers with the answer key at the end of this lesson. Only the words that go in the blanks are given, since everyone will create different sentences. **My score for Exercise 5 is _____ out of 10.**

## VARIATIONS

In Lesson 3, you learned about two-vowel combinations that represent one sound. For example, the word *sea* (meaning the ocean) has two vowels, but the letters *ea* represent only one sound—long /ē/. This is not always the case with two vowels together. Sometimes, when words are broken into syllables between the two vowels, both letters are pronounced. In this case, the first syllable is open and the second syllable begins with a vowel. For example, the word *diet* has two vowels, but also has two syllables. Read the word *diet* as /d /ī/ /ĕ /t/. Read the following words syllable by syllable.

| | |
|---|---|
| po em | po et |
| ri ot | ru in |
| tri o | vid e o |

Another syllable to look closely at is **consonant + *le***. The final letter *e* is silent. Examples of the consonant + *le* syllable include the letters *ble*, as found in the word *table* (/t/ā/b/l/); *cle* as found in the word *circle* (/s/ir/c/l/); *dle*, as found in the word *handle* (/h/ă /n/d/l/); *kle*, as found in the word *ankle* (/ă /n/k/l/); *ple*, as found in the word *people* (/p/ē/p/l/); and *tle*, as found in the word *title* (/t /ī/t/l/). Just remember that with the consonant + *le* relationship, the letter/sound relationship is consistent and the final letter *e* is silent. The following are a few more words to illustrate this syllable.

| | |
|---|---|
| spar**kle** | pur**ple** |
| sta**ble** | **little** |
| can**dle** | gar**gle** |

Note that if you add the letter *r*, as in the word *sparkler*, the letters *er* together make the murmur vowel /er/ so that the *e* is no longer silent.

Spelling words that end in *able* or *ible* can be challenging because both endings sound the same. The *a* in *able* and the *i* in *ible* both have the schwa sound, the sound you hear in the word *of*. Try these *able* and *ible* words if you're ready for the challenge. Call on your study buddy to dictate them to you as you write them in your notebook.

| | | | |
|---|---|---|---|
| pay**able** | account**able** | expand**able** | profit**able** |
| advis**able** | inevit**able** | perish**able** | attain**able** |
| transfer**able** | inexcus**able** | | |

| | | | |
|---|---|---|---|
| respons**ible** | deduct**ible** | convert**ible** | compat**ible** |
| sens**ible** | elig**ible** | | |

## EXERCISE 6: WHAT HAVE YOU LEARNED?

**Directions:** Separate the words into syllables and write whether the vowel in the first syllable is long or short. The first one is done for you.

| Word | Syllables | First Vowel |
|---|---|---|
| **1.** slippery | *slip per y* | *short /ĭ/* |
| **2.** dragon | _____ | _____ |
| **3.** clever | _____ | _____ |
| **4.** bacon | _____ | _____ |
| **5.** robberies | _____ | _____ |
| **6.** vanish | _____ | _____ |
| **7.** silently | _____ | _____ |
| **8.** buttery | _____ | _____ |
| **9.** musical | _____ | _____ |
| **10.** billowing | _____ | _____ |

**Directions:** Write all the words in the following sentences that have three syllables. For added practice, have your study buddy dictate the sentences to you.

**11.** Billowing clouds were sparkling in the sunset.

**12.** The buttery popcorn slipped from her hands.

**13.** The shimmering desert sun beat endlessly on the arid sand.

**14.** The recording studio projected a profit of $3 million.

**15.** The financial advisor hammered out all the minute details of the contract.

**16.** Mr. Butterly, the project manager, refused to take the blame for the stolen batteries.

**17.** The musical interlude prepared us for happier moments.

**18.** The people waited for the jury's decision.

**19.** The police reported no unsolved mysteries for a period of two weeks.

**20.** Let's celebrate Independence Day with sparklers and fireworks.

Check your answers with the answer key at the end of this lesson.

**My score for Exercise 6 is _____ out of 10.**

## ANSWERS

### Exercise 1
**1.** sparkles
**2.** sloppy
**3.** label
**4.** mystery
**5.** music
**6.** desert
**7.** prettier
**8.** billowed
**9.** skinny
**10.** project

### Exercise 2
**1.** 1, 2, 3
**2.** 1, 2, 3
**3.** 1, 2, 3
**4.** 2, 3, 4
**5.** 2, 3, 4

### Exercise 3
**1.** long /ē/
**2.** short /ĕ/
**3.** short /ĭ/
**4.** long /ī/
**5.** short /ĕ/
**6.** long /ē/
**7.** short /ŏ/
**8.** long /ō/

### Exercise 4
**1.** sparklers
**2.** slippery
**3.** labeling
**4.** mysteries
**5.** musical
**6.** deserting
**7.** pretty
**8.** billowing
**9.** skinnier
**10.** projected

### Exercise 5
**1.** slippery
**2.** musical
**3.** mysteries
**4.** deserting
**5.** billowing
**6.** projected

7. labeling
8. pretty
9. skinnier
10. sparklers

## Exercise 6

1. slip per y     short / ĭ /
2. drag on     short / ă /
3. clev er     short / ĕ /
4. ba con     long / ā /
5. rob ber ies     short / ŏ /
6. van ish     short / ă /
7. si lent ly     long / ī /
8. but ter y     short / ŭ /

9. mu si cal     long / ū /
10. bil low ing     short / ĭ /
11. billowing (*Sparkling* is actually only two syllables—spar kling.)
12. buttery
13. shimmering, endlessly
14. recording, studio, projected
15. financial, advisor
16. Butterly, manager, batteries
17. musical, interlude, happier
18. decision
19. reported, mysteries
20. celebrate, fireworks

# LESSON

# 16

# THE BASE WORD

This lesson focuses on the ever-changing base word. As you know, a foundation is something you can build on—and that is exactly what you will do in this lesson as you learn how to build on the base, or foundation, word.

## EXERCISE 1: EYEBALLING SPELLING LIST 16

**Directions:** Sweep your eyes across the line from left to right and back again. Do it quickly. Circle the word in each line that looks different from the others on that line.

Are you ready? Get set . . . Go!

| | | | |
|---|---|---|---|
| **1.** wanted | waited | waited | waited |
| **2.** composed | composed | composed | compiled |
| **3.** played | played | played | player |
| **4.** debts | debits | debits | debits |
| **5.** taxable | taxes | taxes | taxes |
| **6.** bunches | bunches | brunches | bunches |
| **7.** winning | winning | winning | wanting |

|  |  |  |  |
|---|---|---|---|
| **8.** thinking | thinking | thinking | winking |
| **9.** shipped | shipped | shipped | shopped |
| **10.** cashing | clashing | cashing | cashing |

Check your answers with the answer key at the end of this lesson.
**My score for Exercise 1 is** _____ **out of 10.**

## REFLECTION

Go back to the words that are the same in each line. Find the base or foundation word. Now look at the endings attached to each base word. Write all the endings that you see. _____

Why do you think the words have different endings? _____

_____

If you noticed that the words ended with *ing*, *ed*, *es*, and *s*, that's a great start. The words have different endings for a very good reason. Words are usually said or written in context (sentences) that convey meaning. When a word is about an action, the ending of the base word informs the listener or reader about when something is happening. The ending conveys the **tense** (time) of the verb (action word). The tense could be the past (yesterday or last year), present (going on right now), or the future (tomorrow or years from now). It is the base word that conveys the **meaning** and the end that conveys the sense of **when** the base word happened. Keep your eye on the base words *step* and *fax* in the following sentences:

She **steps** on the rocks.　　　He **faxes** the information.
She is **stepping** on the rocks.　He is **faxing** the information.
She **stepped** on the rocks.　　He **faxed** the information.

Can you see and hear how the base word changes?

If the base word refers to a thing—that is, if the base word is a noun—the ending can change to indicate the "number of," or the amount. If the amount is one, it's called **singular**, and if the amount is more than one, it's called **plural**. Keep your eye on the base words *battery*, *box*, and *label* in the following sentences.

The small radio needs one **battery**, but the larger radio needs six **batteries**.

Put all the paper in one **box** and the rest of the materials in several larger **boxes**.

Each folder will get one red **label** and three yellow **labels**.

Can you see and hear how the base word changes?

This is all you need to know for now. Move on to Exercise 2, Sound Inventory, to hear the sounds of these endings so you can continue improving your spelling.

## EXERCISE 2: SOUND INVENTORY

**Directions:** Listen to yourself as you read each group of words aloud. **You must read the words out loud.** The letters and sounds in each group have something in common. Put a circle around the letters that are the same in each group and then write the two letters on the lines provided.

**Group 1**

| waited | filed | jumped |
|--------|--------|--------|
| planted | climbed | spiked |
| loaded | mailed | liked |
| rented | curved | danced |
| lasted | thanked | shaved |

_____

**Group 2**

| brushes | boxes |
|---------|-------|
| dishes | taxes |
| wishes | buzzes |
| lunches | classes |
| speeches | passes |

_____

In Group 1, the common letters are *ed*. Can you hear the sound of the letters *ed*? Group 1 has three sets of words ending with the letters *ed*. That's because the letters *ed* can represent three different sounds. Break all the words into sounds using slash marks. The word *lasted* should look like /l/ă/s/t/e/d/. The word *jumped* should look like /j/ŭ/m/p/t/, and the word *filed* should look like /f/ī/l/d/. Can you hear that the letters *ed* represent the sound of /ě/d/, /t/, and /d/? The *ed* is used to change the tense of a base word to indicate that an action took place in the past.

In Group 2, the common letters are *es*. Can you hear the sound of the letters *es*? Break all the words in Group 2 into sounds using slash marks. The word *brushes* should look like /b/r/ŭ/sh/ě/s/ and the word *boxes* should look like /b/ŏ/k/s/ě/s/. Now can you hear the sound? Remember this general rule:

**The tense and number of words ending with *ch*, *sh*, *s*, *x*, and *z* is changed by adding the letters *es* to the end of the word.**

Other words just take on the letter s as part of the letter/sound relationship when they change tense or number. Using slash marks, the word *label* looks like /l/ā/b/l/, and *labels* looks like /l/ā/b/l/s/.

The rules aren't a necessary part of this lesson as long as you keep the letter/sound relationship. You heard that the letters *ed* can sound like /ě/d/, /t/, or /d/.

You heard /s/ and / ĕ /s/. Keep spelling syllable by syllable and you will keep expanding your pool of spelling words.

## REFLECTION

Why does a word have an ending? _____

_____

What letters in this lesson represent tense? _____
What letters in this lesson so far mean the number of or the amount?

_____

The letters *ed* can represent three sounds. What are the sounds?

_____

    Endings for words used to indicate tense—past, present, or future—are the letters *s*, *es*, *ed*, and *ing*. The number amount—singular or plural—is indicated by the endings *s* and *es*. The letters *ed* represent the sounds /d/, /t/, and / ĕ /d/ (like the male nickname Ed). Move on to Exercise 3 to practice listening for ending sounds.

## EXERCISE 3: PRACTICE WITH ENDINGS

**Directions:** Read each word aloud. Listen carefully for the sound at the end of the word. Write the symbol /d/, /t/, or /ĕ/d/ for the sound you hear. The first few are done for you. Get your study buddy to read the words to you. Try to really focus your listening.

**1.** depleted    /ĕ/d/

| | | | | | | | |
|---|---|---|---|---|---|---|---|
| **2.** ordered | /d/ | **7.** landed | _____ | **12.** played | _____ |
| **3.** thanked | /t/ | **8.** served | _____ | **13.** wished | _____ |
| **4.** raced | _____ | **9.** rented | _____ | **14.** waited | _____ |
| **5.** composed | _____ | **10.** sounded | _____ | **15.** printed | _____ |
| **6.** uplifted | _____ | **11.** touched | _____ | | |

    Check your answers with the answer key at the end of this lesson.
**My score for Exercise 3 is _____ out of 15.**

    Now try a practice exercise that will sharpen your spelling of endings.
**Directions:** Read the words aloud from left to right. Practice writing the words or call on your study buddy to dictate the words to you. It's a good idea to listen to each syllable before you write.

| | | | |
|---|---|---|---|
| touch | touches | touched | touching |
| buzz | buzzes | buzzed | buzzing |
| punch | punches | punched | punching |
| brush | brushes | brushed | brushing |
| fax | faxes | faxed | faxing |
| flex | flexes | flexed | flexing |
| retail | retails | retailed | retailing |
| page | pages | paged | paging |

## EXERCISE 4: PRACTICE WRITING SPELLING LIST 16

**Directions:** Go back to Exercise 1. Look at the three words that are the same on each line. Write each of these words only once on the lines below. This would be a good time to have your study buddy dictate the words to you.

1. _____
2. _____
3. _____
4. _____
5. _____

6. _____
7. _____
8. _____
9. _____
10. _____

Consult your dictionary if the meaning of a word is unfamiliar to you.

Check your answers with the answer key at the end of this lesson.

**My score for Exercise 4 is _____ out of 10.**

## EXERCISE 5: PRACTICE WRITING SPELLING LIST 16 IN CONTEXT

**Directions:** Use the words from Exercise 4 to complete the following phrases. For added practice, rewrite the entire phrase in your own sentence on the provided line.

1. _____ lottery ticket

_____

2. _____ at the bus stop

_____

3. _____ your check

_____

4. _____ via overnight delivery

_____

**5.** _____ carefully on an exam

_____

**6.** _____ on the bank statement

_____

**7.** _____ of fragrant flowers

_____

**8.** pay city and state _____

_____

**9.** _____ music for the lyrics

_____

**10.** _____ my favorite song

_____

Check your answers with the answer key at the end of this lesson. Only the words that go in the blanks are given, since everyone will create different sentences. **My score for Exercise 5 is _____ out of 10.**

## VARIATIONS

Here are the variations of some words when changing them from singular (one) to plural (many).

Some words that end in *f* or *fe* change the *f* or *fe* to the letter *v* and add the letters *es*.

| | | | |
|---|---|---|---|
| leaf | leaves | calf | calves |
| loaf | loaves | half | halves |
| thief | thieves | shelf | shelves |

Some words that end in the vowel *o* add the letter *s* if the *o* is preceded by a vowel, or the letters *es* if the *o* is preceded by a consonant.

| | | | |
|---|---|---|---|
| radio | radios | patio | patios |
| rodeo | rodeos | tomato | tomatoes |
| potato | potatoes | echo | echoes |
| zero | zeroes | veto | vetoes |
| duo | duos | igloo | igloos |

Some words that end with a consonant plus the letter *y* change the *y* to *i* and add *es*.

| | | | |
|---|---|---|---|
| lily | lil**ies** | cherry | cher**ries** |
| pony | pon**ies** | penny | penn**ies** |

Some words that end with a vowel followed by the letter *y* simply take the letter *s*.

| | | | |
|---|---|---|---|
| key | key**s** | tray | tray**s** |
| day | day**s** | turkey | turke**ys** |

The final consonant in the base word is sometimes doubled, as in the next group of words.

| | | |
|---|---|---|
| submi**t** | submit**ted** | submit**ting** |
| shi**p** | ship**ped** | ship**ping** |

The letter/sound relationship doesn't always work when the base word receives an ending. Take out your notebook and practice the words below. Write them many times or in sentences.

Do you want to see more challenging words in different tenses? Try these! Call on your study buddy to dictate them to you as you write them in your notebook.

| | | |
|---|---|---|
| copy | notify | ero**de** |
| cop**ies** | noti**fies** | erode**s** |
| cop**ied** | noti**fied** | erode**d** |
| copy**ing** | notif**ying** | erod**ing** |
| cop**ier** | noti**fication** | eros**ion** |
| | | |
| nod | vary | permi**t** |
| nod**s** | var**ies** | permit**s** |
| nod**ded** | var**ied** | permit**ted** |
| nod**ding** | vari**ation** | permi**ssion** |

# EXERCISE 6: WHAT HAVE YOU LEARNED?

**Directions:** Choose a word that best completes the sentence. For added practice, ask your study buddy to dictate the completed sentences to you. Write them in your notebook.

1. How many _____ will you attend next semester? (class, classes)
2. He _____ the lyrics in the last two years of his life. (composes, composed)
3. The pansies _____ in the garden all summer. (blooms, bloomed)
4. Paying city and state _____ is your responsibility. (taxes, taxed)
5. Chop two _____ of parsley for that salad. (bunches, bunched)
6. The orders were _____ two weeks ago. (submit, submitted)
7. The toddler climbed the _____ and sang a song. (steps, stepping)
8. The team _____ two hours for the rain to stop. (waited, waiting)
9. The gardener planted rose_____ along the slate path. (bush, bushes)
10. The baker removed five _____ of bread from the brick oven. (loaf, loaves)

Check your answers with the answer key at the end of this lesson.
**My score for Exercise 6 is _____ out of 10.**

## ANSWERS

### Exercise 1
1. wanted
2. compiled
3. player
4. debts
5. taxable
6. brunches
7. wanting
8. winking
9. shopped
10. clashing

8. /d/
9. /ĕ/d/
10. /ĕ/d/
11. /t/
12. /d/
13. /t/
14. /ĕ/d/
15. /ĕ/d/

### Exercise 3
1. /ĕ/d/
2. /d/
3. /t/
4. /t/
5. /d/
6. /ĕ/d/
7. /ĕ/d/

### Exercise 4
1. waited
2. composed
3. played
4. debits
5. taxes
6. bunches
7. winning
8. thinking
9. shipped
10. cashing

## Exercise 5

1. winning
2. waited
3. cashing
4. shipped
5. thinking
6. debits
7. bunches
8. taxes
9. composed
10. played

## Exercise 6

1. classes
2. composed
3. bloomed
4. taxes
5. bunches
6. submitted
7. steps
8. waited
9. bushes
10. loaves

# LESSON 17

# GETTING OFF FIRST BASE

New words can be derived from a base word, also known as the **root** word, by adding syllables. Syllables that have a specific meaning are called **prefixes** and **suffixes**. This lesson shows you how to add prefixes and suffixes to base words to increase your pool of spelling words further.

## EXERCISE 1: EYEBALLING SPELLING LIST 17

**Directions:** Sweep your eyes across the line from left to right and back again. Do it quickly. Circle the word in each line that looks different from the others on that line.

Are you ready? Get set . . . Go!

| | | | |
|---|---|---|---|
| **1.** recover | recover | recover | remover |
| **2.** overpasses | overpass | overpass | overpass |
| **3.** prewashing | prewashing | prewashing | presenting |
| **4.** unbreakable | unspeakable | unbreakable | unbreakable |
| **5.** interstate | interstate | interstate | interview |
| **6.** impure | impolite | impolite | impolite |
| **7.** distasteful | distasteful | distasteful | disgraceful |

**8.** mistreatment mistreatment mistreatment misstatement

**9.** informative instructive informative informative

**10.** impossible impassable impassable impassable

Check your answers with the answer key at the end of this lesson.
**My score for Exercise 1 is _____ out of 10.**

## REFLECTION

Go back to the words that are the same in each line. Look at the words very carefully. Remove a syllable at the beginning of each word and remove a syllable at the end of each word. Now look at what's left. The remaining word is called a **base**, or **root**, word. The base word in the word *recover* is *cover*. Try to locate all the other base words.

In the word *unbreakable*, there is a base word, a prefix, and a suffix.

*un* (**prefix**) + *break* (**base**)+ *able* (**suffix**)

You'll learn more about prefixes and suffixes later in this lesson. Move on to Exercise 2, Sound Inventory, to listen for common base words.

## EXERCISE 2: SOUND INVENTORY

**Directions:** Read each group of words aloud and listen for the base word in each group. Write the base word on the line below each group.

| **Group 1** | **Group 2** | **Group 3** |
|---|---|---|
| reaction | uncover | exportation |
| inaction | recovery | transportation |
| interaction | discover | export |
| _____ | | _____ |

| **Group 4** | **Group 5** |
|---|---|
| publication | enjoyable |
| republication | joyous |
| publicly | joyful |
| _____ | _____ |

The base word in Group 1 is *act*. There are three prefixes: *re, in,* and *inter.* The prefixes are spelled exactly as you would expect from the letter/sound relationship.

There is one suffix: *ion*. The letters *ion* represent the sound /sh/ŭ/n/, as you learned in Lesson 14. So, the word *reaction*, represented in sounds, is written as /r/ē/ă/c/sh/ŭ/n/.

The base word in Group 2 is *cover*. There are three prefixes: *un*, *re*, and *dis*. The suffix is *y*. The prefixes are spelled exactly as you would expect from the letter/sound relationship. So the word *discovery*, represented as sounds, is written as /d/ĭ/s/c/ ŏ /v/er/y/.

The base word in Group 3 is *port*. There are two prefixes: *ex* and *trans*. The prefixes are spelled exactly as you would expect from the letter/sound relationship. There is one suffix, *ation*, which is represented in sounds as /ā/sh/ŭ/n/. So the word *exportation*, represented in sounds, is written as / ĕ /k/s/p/or/t/ā/sh/ŭ/n/.

The base word in Group 4 is *public*. There is one prefix, *re*. There are two suffixes: *ation*, represented as /ā/sh/ŭ/n/, and *ly*, represented as /l/ē/, as found in the letter/sound relationship. So the word *republication*, represented by sounds, is written as /r/ē/p/ ŭ /b/l/ĭ/c/ā/sh/ŭ/n/.

The base word in Group 5 is *joy*. There is one prefix: *en*. There are three suffixes: *ful*, which is spelled exactly as you would expect from the letter/sound relationship; *ous*, represented as /ü/s/; and *able*, represented as /ä/b/l/. Therefore, the word *joyous*, represented in sounds, is written /j/oy/ü/s/, and the word *enjoyable* is written as / ĕ /n/j/oy/ä/b/l/. The vowels in *able* and *ous* lose their sound to schwa. (See Lesson 15.)

The syllables added to the beginning of the words are called **prefixes**. They influence the base word because they have meaning. The following is a list of prefixes and their meanings, with clue phrases to help you remember their meanings.

| Prefix | Meaning | Clue Phrase |
|---|---|---|
| *re* | to do again | retesting students |
| *pre* | before | pretest results |
| *mis* | wrong or bad | misspell words |
| *mid* | middle of | midnight snack |
| *ir* | not/opposite of | irrational behavior |
| *im* | not/opposite of | impossible tasks |
| *un* | not/opposite of | unhappy gamblers |
| *in* | not/into | inactive stocks |
| *il* | not/opposite of | illegal handguns |
| *inter* | among, between | interactive groups |

The syllable added to the end of a word is called a **suffix**. Like the prefix, it also adds to the meaning of a base word.

| Prefix | Meaning | Clue Phrase |
|--------|---------|-------------|
| *ful* | full of | joyful |
| *less* | without, free from | careless |
| *ly* | how something is done | expertly |
| *y* | tells what something is like | rocky |
| *en* | what something is made of | golden |
| *able* | tells what something can do or be | passable |
| *ous* | full of or like | dangerous |
| *ism* | act or fact of doing | criticism |
| *ible* | what something can do or be | responsible |

Endings, highlighted in bold below, change a base word to a derivative form.

| Base | Derivative Form | Letter/Sound Relationship |
|------|-----------------|---------------------------|
| elect | elec**tion** | /sh/ŭ/n/ |
| examine | examin**ation** | /ā/sh/ŭ/n/ |
| sculpt | sculp**ture** | /ch/ur/ |
| depend | depend**ence** | /ĕ/n/s/ (schwa vowel) |
| assist | assist**ance** | /ä/n/s/ (schwa vowel) |
| dismiss | dismiss**al** | /ä/l/ (schwa vowel) |

## Prefixes and Suffixes Are Consistent

It's important to remember that most prefixes and suffixes are consistent with the letter/sound relationship strategy. The words you'll be spelling from here on in are multisyllabic, but don't worry, you have the skills to do it. Just spell words beat by beat, syllable by syllable.

## REFLECTION

What can be attached to the beginning and ending of a base word to change its meaning? _____

No matter how many letters long the word is, why will you still be able to spell it correctly? _____

_____

Prefixes and suffixes can be added to a base word to change its meaning. No matter how complex the word is that you're trying to spell, you will be successful. Why? You know about letter/sound relationships, and prefixes and suffixes usually follow this strategy. Always listen syllable by syllable before you attempt to spell a word.

## EXERCISE 3: PRACTICE WITH BASE WORDS

**Directions:** Read each word aloud and write the base word on the provided line.

**1.** overpass     _____

**2.** replacement    _____

**3.** impoliteness   _____

**4.** unmanageable _____

**5.** interviewers   _____

**6.** impassable     _____

**7.** unreasonable  _____

**8.** distrustful     _____

**9.** reaction       _____

**10.** mistreatment  _____

Check your answers with the answer key at the end of this lesson.

**My score for Exercise 3 is \_\_\_\_\_ out of 10.**

## EXERCISE 4: PRACTICE WRITING SPELLING LIST 17

**Directions:** Go back to Exercise 1. Look at the three words that are the same on each line. Write each of these words only once on the lines below. This would be a good time to have your study buddy dictate the words to you.

**1.** _____

**2.** _____

**3.** _____

**4.** _____

**5.** _____

**6.** _____

**7.** _____

**8.** _____

**9.** _____

**10.** _____

Consult your dictionary if the meaning of a word is unfamiliar to you.

Check your answers with the answer key at the end of this lesson.

**My score for Exercise 4 is \_\_\_\_\_ out of 10.**

## EXERCISE 5: PRACTICE WRITING SPELLING LIST 17 IN CONTEXT

**Directions:** Use the words from Exercise 4 to complete the following phrases. For added practice, rewrite the entire phrase in your own sentence on the provided line.

**1.** _____ highway

_____

**2.** _____ from the flu

_____

**3.** _____ of the prisoners

_____

**4.** an _____, icy highway

_____

**5.** _____ dirty dishes

_____

**6.** _____ plastic dishes

_____

**7.** the _____ crosses the highway

_____

**8.** _____ behavior in front of the family

_____

**9.** an _____ guidebook

_____

**10.** _____ and without manners

_____

Check your answers with the answer key at the end of this lesson. Only the words that go in the blanks are given, since everyone will create different sentences. **My score for Exercise 5 is _____ out of 10.**

## VARIATIONS

The following words contain prefixes and suffixes. These prefixes and suffixes are used less often than the others you have studied so far, but they're still important—and they're easy to spell because they never change.

The following are words with the prefix *super*, meaning *above*, *over*, or *at the top of*.

**super**man    **super**ego    **super**human
**super**impose    **super**natural

The following are words with the prefix *sub*, meaning *under* or *below*.

**sub**conscious    **sub**contract    **sub**sidiary

The following are words with the suffixes *er* and *ist*. These two endings indicate a person somehow associated with the root word.

| | | | |
|---|---|---|---|
| perfection**ist** | thera**pist** | build**er** | design**er** |
| capital**ist** | radiolog**ist** | dwell**er** | biograph**er** |
| audiolog**ist** | | vacation**er** | |

There are many other prefixes and suffixes.

Do you want more challenging words? Try these! Call on your study buddy to dictate them to you as you write them in your notebook.

Words in this challenge have the suffixes *ence* and *ance*. The challenge is that they both sound similar. In these two prefixes, the vowels take on the schwa sound.

| *ence* | *ance* |
|---|---|
| audience | admittance |
| interdependence | hindrance |
| benevolence | allowance |
| convalescence | utterance |
| reference | appearance |
| | clearance |

## EXERCISE 6: WHAT HAVE YOU LEARNED?

**Directions:** Read each phrase aloud. Locate the base word that has both a prefix and a suffix. Write only the base word on the line next to the phrase. It would be good practice to have your study buddy dictate these phrases to you.

**1.** disorderly conduct _____

**2.** citywide transportation _____

**3.** a biweekly payment _____

**4.** unreasonable behavior _____

**5.** thinking irrationally _____

**6.** interchangeable parts _____

**7.** unmanageable children _____

**8.** a disagreeable person _____

**9.** an interactive computer _____

**10.** an unprintable news account _____

Check your answers with the answer key at the end of this lesson.

**My score for Exercise 6 is _____ out of 10.**

## ANSWERS

### Exercise 1

1. remover
2. overpasses
3. presenting
4. unspeakable
5. interview
6. impure
7. disgraceful
8. misstatement
9. instructive
10. impossible

8. mistreatment
9. informative
10. impassable

### Exercise 5

1. interstate
2. recover
3. mistreatment
4. impassable
5. prewashing
6. unbreakable
7. overpass
8. distasteful
9. informative
10. impolite

### Exercise 3

1. pass
2. place
3. polite
4. manage
5. view
6. pass
7. reason
8. trust
9. act
10. treat

### Exercise 6

1. order
2. port
3. week (*Payment* has only a suffix.)
4. reason
5. rational
6. change
7. manage
8. agree
9. act
10. print

### Exercise 4

1. recover
2. overpass
3. prewashing
4. unbreakable
5. interstate
6. impolite
7. distasteful

# LESSON 18

# SPELLING DEMONS

This lesson contains common and uncommon words that give spellers a hard time. We call them "spelling demons." What makes them so difficult is that they have no pattern. However, using the letter/sound relationship strategy will help you find those silent letters that just "hold a place."

### EXERCISE 1: EYEBALLING SPELLING LIST 18

**Directions:** Sweep your eyes across the line from left to right and back again. Do it quickly. Circle the word in each line that looks different from the others on that line.

Are you ready? Get set . . . Go!

| | | | |
|---|---|---|---|
| **1.** subtle | subtle | subtle | subtitle |
| **2.** beauty | beauty | beauty | beautify |
| **3.** jeopardize | jeopardy | jeopardy | jeopardy |
| **4.** columns | clowns | columns | columns |
| **5.** answer | anther | answer | answer |
| **6.** freed | friend | friend | friend |
| **7.** honest | honest | honest | hone |

**157**

|   |   |   |   |
|---|---|---|---|
| **8.** island | island | island | inland |
| **9.** asthma | asthma | asthma | asterisk |
| **10.** acquire | acquaint | acquaint | acquaint |

Check your answers with the answer key at the end of this lesson.

**My score for Exercise 1 is _____ out of 10.**

## REFLECTION

Go back to the words that are the same on each line. Look at the words carefully. Which ones are a real spelling challenge for you?

_____

The words in this lesson don't have a sound pattern or common letters. That's why they are called "spelling demons." Move on to Exercise 2, Sound Inventory, to locate the silent letters that "just hold a place."

## EXERCISE 2: SOUND INVENTORY

**Directions:** Read the words aloud. The words written using the letter/sound relationship will help you locate the silent letter or letters. Write the silent letter or letters on the provided space. The first one is done for you.

| | | |
|---|---|---|
| **1.** subtle | /s/ŭ/t/l/ | _b_ |
| **2.** beauty | /b/ū/t/ē/ | _____ |
| **3.** jeopardy | /j/ĕ/p/ar/d/ē/ | _____ |
| **4.** columns | /c/ŏ/l/ŭ/m/s/ | _____ |
| **5.** answer | /ă/n/s/er/ | _____ |
| **6.** honest | /ŏ/n/ĕ/s/t/ | _____ |
| **7.** island | /ĭ/l/ă/n/d/ | _____ |
| **8.** asthma | /ă/z/m/ä/ | _____ |
| **9.** acquaint | /ă/k/w/ā/n/t/ | _____ |
| **10.** friend | /f/r/ĕ/n/d/ | _____ |

Check your answers with the answer key at the end of the lesson.

**My score for Exercise 2 is _____ out of 10.**

# EXERCISE 3: PRACTICE WITH SPELLING DEMONS

**Directions:** Read the words aloud. Then write the base word on the provided line.

**1.** doubtful _____
**2.** answerable _____
**3.** columnist _____
**4.** friendly _____
**5.** friendless _____

**6.** islander _____
**7.** friendship _____
**8.** unanswerable _____
**9.** unfriendly _____
**10.** doubtfully _____

Check your answers with the answer key at the end of this lesson.
**My score for Exercise 3 is _____ out of 10.**

# EXERCISE 4: PRACTICE WRITING SPELLING LIST 18

**Directions:** Go back to Exercise 1. Look at the three words that are the same on each line. Write each of these words only once on the lines below. This would be a good time to have your study buddy dictate the words to you.

**1.** _____
**2.** _____
**3.** _____
**4.** _____
**5.** _____

**6.** _____
**7.** _____
**8.** _____
**9.** _____
**10.** _____

Consult your dictionary if the meaning of a word is unfamiliar to you.
Check your answers with the answer key at the end of this lesson.
**My score for Exercise 4 is _____ out of 10.**

# EXERCISE 5: PRACTICE WRITING SPELLING LIST 18 IN CONTEXT

**Directions:** Use the words from Exercise 4 to complete the following phrases. For added practice, rewrite the entire phrase in your own sentence on the provided line.

**1.** _____ the question

_____

**2.** _____ attack

_____

**3.** a tropical _____ resort

_____

**4.** an _____ response

_____

**5.** a trustworthy _____

_____

**6.** _____ on the front of a building

_____

**7.** the _____ of a sunset

_____

**8.** _____ yourself with a new friend

_____

**9.** _____ gesture

_____

**10.** in danger or _____

_____

Check your answers with the answer key at the end of this lesson. Only the words that go in the blanks are given, since everyone will create different sentences. **My score for Exercise 5 is _____ out of 10.**

## VARIATIONS

In the following spelling demons, the base word changes when an ending is added. Notice how the final letters are usually dropped or changed when the suffix is added.

| | | | |
|---|---|---|---|
| jeopardy | jeopard**ize** | | |
| beauty | beaut**ify** | beaut**iful** | beautif**ication** |
| efficient | efficien**cy** | | |
| acquaint | acquaint**ance** | | |
| acquire | acqui**sition** | | |

Do you want more challenging words? Read each of the following phrases aloud. Each underlined word is a spelling demon you should practice. These are more difficult than the first ten you learned. When you're sure you can spell these words, call on your study buddy to dictate the phrases to you.

succeeded in big **business**
a fruit and **vegetable** market
**lieutenant** in the Navy
a **souvenir** from Holland
your driver's **license**
a cash register **receipt**
a **convenience** store
the Teamster's **union**

**maneuver** the car into place
a **psychic** reader
**foreign** students
**sophomore** in high school
ill with **pneumonia**
**Wednesday** afternoon
daily **exercise**

## EXERCISE 6: WHAT HAVE YOU LEARNED?

**Directions:** Complete each sentence with the correct form of the word.

**1.** Her smile was so _____ that I didn't notice it at first. (subtle, subtly)
**2.** Your best _____ will comfort you. (friend, friendship)
**3.** It's hard to find people who are so _____ that they will admit their mistakes. (honest, honestly)
**4.** The soft light enhanced the model's _____. (beauty, beautiful)
**5.** Walking on railroad tracks will put your life in _____. (jeopardize, jeopardy)
**6.** Unfortunately, he has had _____ since he was a young boy, which has made it difficult for him to participate in sports. (asthmatic, asthma)
**7.** _____ of smoke billowed from the chimney. (Columns, Columnist)
**8.** Farming and tourism supported the people on the _____. (island, islanders)
**9.** You must _____ yourself with the information before you speak. (acquire, acquaint)
**10.** What is your _____ to the question? (answerable, answer)

Check your answers with the answer key at the end of this lesson.
**My score for Exercise 6 is _____ out of 10.**

# ANSWERS

## Exercise 1
1. subtitle
2. beautify
3. jeopardize
4. clowns
5. anther
6. freed
7. hone
8. inland
9. asterisk
10. acquire

## Exercise 2
1. b
2. ea
3. o
4. n
5. w
6. h
7. s
8. th
9. c
10. i

## Exercise 3
1. doubt
2. answer
3. column
4. friend
5. friend
6. island
7. friend
8. answer
9. friend
10. doubt

## Exercise 4
1. subtle
2. beauty
3. jeopardy
4. columns
5. answer
6. friend
7. honest
8. island
9. asthma
10. acquaint

## Exercise 5
1. answer
2. asthma
3. island
4. honest
5. friend
6. columns
7. beauty
8. acquaint
9. subtle
10. jeopardy

## Exercise 6
1. subtle
2. friend
3. honest
4. beauty
5. jeopardy
6. asthma
7. Columns
8. island
9. acquaint
10. answer

# LESSON

# 19

# TRENDY WORDS AND MIXED PAIRS

The English language is a flexible one. New words are being introduced continually to help us communicate about societal changes, technological advances, and so on. Sometimes, the words themselves aren't new, but they take on a new meaning. This lesson introduces categories of words or phrases that reflect a **trend**, as well as words known as **mixed pairs**.

## EXERCISE 1: BECOMING FAMILIAR WITH TRENDY WORDS

**Directions:** Read each category of words. Pay careful attention to those that are underlined, and write them in the margin or make a list in your notebook. You'll be using them in a later exercise.

**Words for Health**

artificial sweetener

beta carotene

holistic medicine

fat free

cholesterol

carbohydrates

protein

**Words for Technology**

<u>cell</u> phone, cellular

online, computer

hard drive

key<u>board</u>, font

laser printer

scanner

video, video camera

## Words for Health (cont.)

spinning

personal trainer, physical therapy

juicer, juice machine

Pilates

pita bread

## Words for Civil Service Employees

mail carrier (replaced *mailman*)

overnight express <u>mail</u>

priority mail

police officer (replaced *policeman*)

bias attack

child abuse

sexual harassment

firefighter (replaced *fireman*)

## Words for Politics and Society

global warming

landfill <u>site</u>

sewage treatment

bottled water

compost, vermicomposting

<u>waste</u> management

## Words for Technology (cont.)

<u>byte</u>, megabyte

modem

satellite, satellite dish

cable television, <u>Weather</u> Channel

surfing the Internet

## Words for Finance

junk bonds

automated teller machine (ATM)

home equity loan

individual retirement account (IRA)

<u>capital</u> gains

premium card

instant cash access

homeowner's insurance

smoke inhalation

## Words for the Environment

in vitro fertilization

genetic engineering

paradigm shift

proactive/reactive

stepfamily

sport utility vehicle

## EXERCISE 2: UNDERSTANDING TRENDY WORDS

**Directions:** Use a word or phrase from the **Technology** category to best complete each sentence.

1. There are more than 100 _____ _____ channels.
2. Hook up the _____ to the telephone line.
3. A wireless phone is a _____ _____.
4. Copies from the _____ _____ are crisp and clear.
5. The greeting cards were printed in a Gothic _____.

**Directions:** Use a correct word or phrase from the **Health** category to best complete each sentence.

**6.** Sugar is being replaced by an _____ _____.

**7.** A round, pocketlike bread is known as a _____.

**8.** After the surgery, you'll need _____ _____ to strengthen your leg muscles.

**9.** _____ _____ is a less conventional type of medical treatment.

**10.** Research suggests that large doses of _____ _____ will reduce the risk of some cancers.

**Directions:** Use a correct word or phrase from the **Civil Service** and **Finance** categories to best complete each sentence.

**11.** _____ _____ protects a family in the case of a fire or other disaster.

**12.** Even though the firefighters were protected, they still suffered from _____ _____.

**13.** You can withdraw cash from a bank any time of the day if you use the _____ _____ _____.

**14.** An _____ _____ _____ will guarantee money for your retirement.

**15.** Use _____ _____ _____ if you want that package delivered tomorrow.

**Directions:** Use a correct word or phrase from the **Politics and Society** and **Environment** categories to best complete each sentence.

**16.** _____ _____ can greatly alter the inheritance traits of future generations.

**17.** The Sanitation Department ships garbage to a _____ almost daily.

**18.** Is _____ _____ safer to drink than tap water?

**19.** Autumn leaves become _____ for the spring planting.

**20.** To respond emotionally is reactive. To respond using a sequential thought process is _____.

Check your answers with the answer key at the end of this lesson. In your notebook, write the words from each list that you would like to learn.

**My score for Exercise 2 is _____ out of 20.**

## REFLECTION

What was your score for Exercise 2? _____

Did you have to look at the list on pages 163–164 to spell the answers correctly?

_____

Write the words or phrases that you need to practice. _____

_____

You could probably spell most of the words correctly in Exercise 2. However, it is likely that you need practice on a few of them. In the next exercise, it's up to you to decide which words you'd like to study.

## EXERCISE 3: SELECTING YOUR OWN SPELLING WORDS

**Directions:** From the results of Exercise 2 and the list on pages 163–164, select ten words you need to practice. Write them on the following lines.

1. _____          6. _____
2. _____          7. _____
3. _____          8. _____
4. _____          9. _____
5. _____         10. _____

Of course, if you need to study more than ten words, go ahead and do so. Don't be overwhelmed by a long list—take it one chunk at a time.

## EXERCISE 4: PRACTICE WRITING SPELLING LIST 19 IN CONTEXT

**Directions:** Write a sentence for each word you chose in Exercise 3. Try to put more than one word in a sentence. For example: The _firefighters_ were treated for _smoke inhalation._

1. _____
2. _____
3. _____
4. _____
5. _____
6. _____
7. _____

**8.** _____

**9.** _____

**10.** _____

## EXERCISE 5: READING THE MIXED PAIRS

**Directions:** Read the following pairs of words aloud. You'll discover that they sound the same. Do you know why they're spelled differently? Consult your dictionary for the answer to that question.

| | | | |
|---|---|---|---|
| sell, cell | byte, bite | weather, whether | for, four |
| mail, male | whole, hole | capital, capitol | site, sight |
| board, bored | waste, waist | | |

These mixed pairs of words are often confused because they sound the same but have different meanings. There are many more of these in the English language. Most of these were chosen from the list on pages 163–164. Reread each pair of words, and this time think of the letter/sound relationships as you read them. Are they consistent with the skills you learned in this book?

## VARIATIONS

The following are more mixed pairs. How many of these are you familiar with already? Use your dictionary to see how spelling changes meaning.

| | | |
|---|---|---|
| base, bass | stationary, stationery | poor, pour, pore |
| hair, hare | peace, piece | right, write |
| seen, scene | break, brake | course, coarse |
| through, threw | principal, principle | there, their, they're |

Do you want more challenging mixed pairs? Try these! Your study buddy can't dictate them to you this time. Because they sound the same, you wouldn't know which word to write! After you consult your dictionary just to be sure of the meanings, write each word in a sentence to cement the meaning in your mind.

| | | |
|---|---|---|
| assent, ascent | cannon, canon | cord, chord |
| council, counsel | compliment, complement | |

## EXERCISE 6: WHAT HAVE YOU LEARNED?

**Directions:** Complete each sentence with the correct word. Once you've filled in the blanks, have your study buddy dictate the completed sentences to you.

1. The _____ phone will _____ for $50. (sell, cell)

2. The newspaper was _____ for stating that the landfill _____ was a _____ for sore eyes. (sight, site, cited)

3. We were all tired and _____ at the community school _____ meeting. (board, bored)

4. The _____ report is uncertain. We don't know _____ to remain home or leave. (weather, whether)

5. Is the state _____ building the location of the vote on the _____ gains tax? (capital, capitol)

6. It's all right to _____ some of your dinner. If you eat too much, it will go right to your _____. (waist, waste)

7. The _____ delivery is expected at noon. (mail, male)

8. The courier will deliver the packages at _____ p.m. (for, four)

9. The computer's memory is measured in _____. (bites, bytes)

10. Who took a _____ out of my pita? (bite, byte)

Check your answers with the answer key at the end of this lesson.
**My score for Exercise 6 is _____ out of 10.**

## ANSWERS

### Exercise 2

1. cable television
2. modem
3. cell phone
4. laser printer
5. font
6. artificial sweetener
7. pita
8. physical therapy
9. Holistic medicine
10. beta carotene
11. Homeowner's insurance
12. smoke inhalation
13. automated teller machine
14. individual retirement account
15. overnight express mail
16. Genetic engineering
17. landfill site
18. bottled water
19. compost
20. proactive

## Exercise 6

1. cell, sell
2. cited, site, sight
3. bored, board
4. weather, whether
5. capitol, capital
6. waste, waist
7. mail
8. four
9. bytes
10. bite

# LESSON

# 20

# PUTTING IT ALL TOGETHER

This lesson is a review of all the lessons you have covered in this book. You'll get the opportunity to practice spelling many of the words you have learned and see which ones you still need to work on.

## WHAT YOU'VE LEARNED

Congratulations! You've traveled a long way from Lesson 1. You should be a great speller by now. Review the lesson summaries below and see if there are any areas you feel you need to go back to.

- The lessons in this book provided you with a keen visual sense about the similarities and differences of words. This was accomplished through the **Eyeballing** exercises. For example, you saw there was a small visual difference between the words *conversation* and *conservation*.
- The lessons also provided you with a keen auditory sense about the sameness of sounds in words. This was accomplished through the **Sound Inventory** exercises. You heard the sameness the words *oyster* and *oil*.
- Through practice with compound words, you picked up an important spelling skill. You learned that putting together two words spells one com-

plex word. Bringing two words together is an easy skill to master, and it expands your pool of spelling words. *Silverware* and *housekeeper* are examples of compound words.

- The lessons provided you with the letter/sound relationship strategy. You now know that letters represent sounds and sounds represent the language you want to write. Thus, the word *starve* can be heard as /s/t/ar/v/ and the word *remember* can be heard as /r/ē/m/ĕ/m/b/er/.

- You learned about hearing the rhythm of language by listening for the number of beats or syllables in a word. There are two syllables in the word *reject* and three in *rejection*.

- You also learned that stress can change the meaning and the form of a word. You know the difference between *des′ ert* and *de sert′*.

- The lessons provided you with the knowledge that the endings *s*, *es*, *ing*, and *ed* can tell the tense of a sentence, as in the words *jumps*, *brushes*, *waiting*, and *stayed*. The endings for the **amount** or **number of** are *s*, *es*, or *ies*, as in words like *keys*, *taxes*, and *stories*.

- You learned the important skill of focusing on the base word and building from it. **Prefixes** and **suffixes** are added to a base word to derive meaning. For instance, the base word *place* can be changed to *replace*, *replacement*, *displace*, and *replaceable*.

- You should now be aware of the importance of **context**, which can tell you the meaning and, therefore, the correct spelling of a word. Words such as *no/know* and *made/maid* are known as **mixed pairs**. The words sound alike and follow the letter/sound relationship patterns, but it's the context that ultimately decides the correct form of the mixed pair.

- You also learned that some words just do **not** follow a pattern or the letter/sound relationship. These "spelling demons" can only be conquered by practice and memorization.

There is an appendix in this book that will help you even more. It contains a complete list of spelling words in this book in alphabetical order, as well as a separate list of spelling demons.

Move on to the final exercises to check your spelling skills.

## REVIEW EXERCISE 1

**Directions:** Read the words on each line from left to right. Circle the word that's misspelled in each line. Write the correct spelling in your notebook.

| | | | |
|---|---|---|---|
| **1.** agents | aquaint | answer | bandstand |
| **2.** bangs | bartend | battere | billowing |
| **3.** beauty | beautifi | bold | boycott |
| **4.** bridge | bushes | bunches | selebrate |
| **5.** crums | cherish | cargo | charmer |
| **6.** dewdrop | classes | conceev | conclusion |
| **7.** cracker | county | country | duble |
| **8.** tasteful | dwells | decision | colums |
| **9.** deserting | composed | expresson | explore |
| **10.** fertile | frend | evolution | emission |

Check your answers with the answer key at the end of this lesson.

**My score for Exercise 1 is _____ out of 10.**

## REVIEW EXERCISE 2

**Directions:** Read the words on each line from left to right. Circle the word that's misspelled in each line. Write the correct spelling in your notebook.

| | | | |
|---|---|---|---|
| **1.** furnishes | gems | gelatin | graphefruit |
| **2.** girl | gnaws | holistik | inlet |
| **3.** impassable | interstayt | lottery | impolite |
| **4.** labeling | leef | limps | lodges |
| **5.** joepardy | keepsake | knit | known |
| **6.** inspection | informative | lumber | misson |
| **7.** oisters | overpass | market | magic |
| **8.** palace | pashun | phantom | memory |
| **9.** photocopy | projected | pheesant | pawns |
| **10.** qualify | qiet | quit | raindrops |

Check your answers with the answer key at the end of this lesson.

**My score for Exercise 2 is _____ out of 10.**

## REVIEW EXERCISE 3

**Directions:** Read the words in each line from left to right. Circle the word that's misspelled in each line. Write the correct spelling in your notebook.

|   | | | |
|---|---|---|---|
| **1.** refund | rodeos | rythms | rhombus |
| **2.** rouf | rough | rowboat | recover |
| **3.** shelf | smuge | slippers | slippery |
| **4.** sparklers | spread | speres | starchy |
| **5.** stitch | stylish | shivver | shorten |
| **6.** swinging | staff | stormy | stilish |
| **7.** unbreakible | thankful | upset | ushers |
| **8.** taxes | therapy | theatrical | sunlite |
| **9.** vertical | voyceless | whenever | wheel |
| **10.** waited | wrist | whisle | wrestling |

Check your answers with the answer key at the end of this lesson.
**My score for Exercise 3 is _____ out of 10.**

You've come a long way since Lesson 1. You've done a great job of putting it all together. Although this is the end of the book, it's not the end of your spelling exercises. Becoming a better speller is a lifelong process. Here are a few suggestions for continuing to improve your skills:

- Keep your notebook active. Refer to it. Add to it.
- Pay attention to the written word no matter where you are. Eyeball advertisements on trains, buses, billboards, newspapers, store windows, menus, and supermarket flyers. Let no word escape you.
- There is one last message for you—be word conscious!

## ANSWERS

### Exercise 1

**1.** aquaint (acquaint)
**2.** battere (battery)
**3.** beautifi (beautify)
**4.** selebrate (celebrate)
**5.** crums (crumbs)
**6.** conceev (conceive)
**7.** duble (double)
**8.** colums (columns)
**9.** expresson (expression)
**10.** frend (friend)

## Exercise 2

1. graphefruit (grapefruit)
2. holistik (holistic)
3. interstayt (interstate)
4. leef (leaf)
5. joepardy (jeopardy)
6. misson (mission)
7. oisters (oysters)
8. pashun (passion)
9. pheesant (pheasant)
10. qiet (quiet)

## Exercise 3

1. rythms (rhythms)
2. rouf (rough)
3. smuge (smudge)
4. speres (spheres)
5. shivver (shiver)
6. stilish (stylish)
7. unbreakible (unbreakable)
8. sunlite (sunlight)
9. voyceless (voiceless)
10. whisle (whistle)

## POSTTEST

Take the following posttest to see how much you've learned. If you think the word is spelled correctly, put a check in the "Correct" column. If you think the word is spelled incorrectly, put a check in the "Incorrect" column. Check your answers against the answer key that follows. The first one has been done for you.

| Word | Correct | Incorrect |
|------|---------|-----------|
| **1.** stilish | | ✓ |
| **2.** selebrate | | |
| **3.** extract | | |
| **4.** naws | | |
| **5.** ushers | | |
| **6.** thirtee | | |
| **7.** weel | | |
| **8.** swinging | | |
| **9.** quill | | |
| **10.** tuffen | | |
| **11.** sentury | | |
| **12.** knit | | |
| **13.** remembers | | |
| **14.** awthor | | |
| **15.** orfan | | |
| **16.** hanset | | |
| **17.** laptop | | |
| **18.** cargo | | |
| **19.** stern | | |
| **20.** computer | | |
| **21.** payeday | | |
| **22.** croud | | |
| **23.** rowbote | | |
| **24.** permit | | |
| **25.** wiker | | |
| **26.** recover | | |
| **27.** winning | | |
| **28.** nashun | | |
| **29.** onest | | |
| **30.** modem | | |
| **31.** pita | | |

| Word | Correct | Incorrect |
|------|---------|-----------|
| **32.** interstate | | |
| **33.** aszma | | |
| **34.** dwells | | |
| **35.** shiped | | |
| **36.** simplification | | |
| **37.** prety | | |
| **38.** musikal | | |
| **39.** depleet | | |
| **40.** dewdrop | | |

## ANSWERS

Here are the posttest answers. Next to each word, you will find listed the lesson number in which it appears.

| Word | Correct | Incorrect |
|------|---------|-----------|
| **1.** stilish (Lesson 7) | | ✓ |
| **2.** selebrate (Lesson 10) | | ✓ |
| **3.** extract (Lesson 11) | ✓ | |
| **4.** naws (Lesson 12) | | ✓ |
| **5.** ushers (Lesson 7) | ✓ | |
| **6.** thirtee (Lesson 8) | | ✓ |
| **7.** weel (Lesson 8) | | ✓ |
| **8.** swinging (Lesson 9) | ✓ | |
| **9.** quill (Lesson 11) | ✓ | |
| **10.** tuffen (Lesson 9) | | ✓ |
| **11.** sentury (Lesson 10) | | ✓ |
| **12.** knit (Lesson 12) | ✓ | |
| **13.** remembers (Lesson 1) | ✓ | |
| **14.** awthor (Lesson 4) | | ✓ |
| **15.** orfan (Lesson 5) | | ✓ |
| **16.** hanset (Lesson 2) | | ✓ |
| **17.** laptop (Lesson 2) | ✓ | |
| **18.** cargo (Lesson 5) | ✓ | |
| **19.** stern (Lesson 6) | ✓ | |
| **20.** computer (Lesson 1) | ✓ | |
| **21.** payeday (Lesson 3) | | ✓ |

| Word | Correct | Incorrect |
|---|---|---|
| **22.** croud (Lesson 4) | | ✓ |
| **23.** rowbote (Lesson 3) | | ✓ |
| **24.** permit (Lesson 6) | ✓ | |
| **25.** wiker (Lesson 13) | | ✓ |
| **26.** recover (Lesson 17) | ✓ | |
| **27.** winning (Lesson 16) | ✓ | |
| **28.** nashun (Lesson 14) | | ✓ |
| **29.** onest (Lesson 18) | | ✓ |
| **30.** modem (Lesson 19) | ✓ | |
| **31.** pita (Lesson 19) | ✓ | |
| **32.** interstate (Lesson 17) | ✓ | |
| **33.** aszma (Lesson 18) | | ✓ |
| **34.** dwells (Lesson 13) | ✓ | |
| **35.** shiped (Lesson 16) | | ✓ |
| **36.** simplification (Lesson 14) | ✓ | |
| **37.** prety (Lesson 15) | | ✓ |
| **38.** musikal (Lesson 15) | | ✓ |
| **39.** deplete (Lesson 1) | ✓ | |
| **40.** dewdrop (Lesson 3) | ✓ | |

# APPENDIX

# MASTER SPELLING LIST

This alphabetical list contains the words from Exercise 1 in Lessons 1–19. It also contains the words listed under **Variations** and **Challenge**. Use this list as a quick reference and as a study guide for practice and review.

| | | |
|---|---|---|
| account | aerobics | always |
| accountable | affirmation | announce |
| acknowledgment | agents | annoyance |
| acquaint | airport | answer |
| acquaintance | allowance | apathy |
| acquire | almost | appearance |
| acquisition | already | applause |
| admission | alteration | aquatic |
| admittance | although | armory |
| advisable | altogether | article |

ascent

assent

asthma

athletes

attainable

attorney

audience

audiologist

auditorium

August

author

authority

automated

automatically

average

awkward


badge

bandstand

bare

bargain

bartend

base

bass

batch

beanbag

bear

beautification

beautiful

beautify

beauty

bedpan

bedspread

believe

benevolence

benign

beta

billowing

biographer


birth

biscuit

bites

board

boisterous

bold

book

bookkeeper

bored

bottled

boulder

boycott

brake

bread

breadbasket

break

bridge

brilliant

brochure

budge

build

builder

bunches

business

byte


cable

calf

calves

campaign

campfire

candle

cannon

canon

capital

capitalist

capitol

care

cargo


carnival

carotene

cashing

catch

ceiling

celebrate

cell

cellophane

cell phone

cellular

cement

cemetery

centerpiece

century

chalk

chamois

channel

charmer

chef

chemical

chemotherapy

chenille

cherish

cherries

cherry

chic

chief

chime

chivalry

cholera

cholesterol

chord

chorus

chromosome

cite

classification

classmate

clearance

cloister

cold

color

columns

commission

compartment

compatible

complement

compliment

composed

composition

compost

compound

compression

compressor

computer

conceive

conclusion

concussion

confusion

constitution

convalescence

convenience

convertible

copied

copier

copies

copy

copying

cord

council

counsel

country

county

couple

course

cracker

creditworthy

crook

crowd

crumbs

curtain

customer

cylinder

dancing

dare

daughter

day

days

dead

deadbeat

deaf

debit

December

decimate

decision

deductible

defamation

departure

deplete

depletion

depression

deserting

design

designer

dewpoint

discharge

discussion

disguise

dishrag

distasteful

ditch

doorway

dormitory

double

dough

dread

duo

duos

Dutch

dweller

dwell

echo

echoes

edge

efficiency

efficient

eight

either

eligible

emergency

emission

employment

engineering

enjoyment

enough

equalization

equipment

equity

erode

eroded

erodes

eroding

erosion

evolution

exact

exceed

except

excerpt

exchange

exercise

exhale

exhaust

exhibit

existence

exonerate

expandable

expect

expensive

experiment

exploit

explore

export

expound

expression

external

extract

extraction

fair

fallen

familiar

fasten

feather

featherbed

fertile

fetch

fixate

floor

fold

for

foreign

fortitude

foundling

four

friend

fudge

furnishes

fusion

gangplank

gargle

gelatin

gems

general

generate

generosity

genetic

genocide

Germany

germicidal

get

ghastly

ghostly

ghostwriter

ghoulish

gimmick

girl

gnaws

gold

gore

grapefruit

graphic

graphite

grasshopper

group

grudge

guardianship

guess

guidance

guide

guitar

gymnasium

gyp

gypsy

hair

half

hallway

halter

halves

handset

hard drive

hare

harpoon

harassment

hatch

head

health

hedge

heinous

heir

hemisphere

hey

high

hindrance

hitch

hold

holistic

honest

honeydew

honeysuckle

hood

hook

hotdog

hutch

igloo

igloos

illusion

impassable

implore

impolite

impression

individual

inevitable

inexcusable

informative

inhalation

innocent

inspection

installation

institution

interdependence
internship
interstate
invitation
island

jeopardize
jeopardy
judge

keepsake
key
keyboard
keys
knighthood
knit
knowledge
knuckle

labeling
landfill
landlord
laptop
laser printer
latch
leaf
leaves
ledge
leisure
license
lieutenant
lilies
lily
limbs
listen
little
loaf
loaves
lodge

look
lore
lottery
lumber
lunch

machine
mail
male
mall
maneuver
market
match
matter
meant
medicine
memory
mess
mission
mistreatment
modem
moist
moisten
moisture
mold
more
mortar
mourn
mummification
musical
mysteries
mystery

nation
nationalization
neighbor
neither
niece
nod

nodded
nods
normal
notification
notified
notifies
notify
notifying

obey
omission
online
oration
orchestra
organist
organization
orphan
overnight
overpass
oversight
overweight
overwhelm
oxide
oxygen
oysters

palace
pamphlet
paradigm
participation
party
passbook
passion
passkey
password
patio
patios
pawns
payable

| | | |
|---|---|---|
| payday | ponies | receive |
| peace | poor | recess |
| peanut | popcorn | recover |
| peculiar | pore | reference |
| pennies | potato | refrigerator |
| penny | potatoes | refund |
| percussion | poultry | regardless |
| perfectionist | pour | rejoice |
| peripheral | precision | relief |
| perishable | pretty | relieve |
| permission | prewashing | remarkable |
| permit | principal | remembers |
| permits | principle | rendition |
| permitted | printer | reservation |
| personal | proactive | responsible |
| personnel | process | restitution |
| phantom | profitable | retirement |
| pheasant | projected | revenge |
| phone | protein | rhetorical |
| phosphorus | provision | rheumatism |
| photocopy | psychic | rhinestone |
| phrase | purchase | rhinoceros |
| physical | purple | rhombus |
| piece | | rhythms |
| pita | qualify | ridge |
| pitch | quicksand | right |
| played | quiet | riot |
| pleasant | quill | rodeo |
| pledge | quintet | rodeos |
| plunger | quit | rough |
| pneumonia | quite | roughneck |
| pocket | | router |
| poem | radio | rowboat |
| poet | radiologist | royalty |
| pointers | radios | ruin |
| poison | raindrops | |
| police | ready | Sabbath |
| pollution | rebate | salesperson |
| pony | receipt | salt |

| | | |
|---|---|---|
| satellite | slippery | subtle |
| sawdust | sludge | sunlight |
| scald | small | superego |
| scanner | smoke | superhuman |
| scene | smudge | superimpose |
| scheduled | snitch | superman |
| scold | snore | supernatural |
| score | snowfall | supervision |
| scratch | sold | sweat |
| seen | sophomore | sweatband |
| seize | soup | sweatshop |
| sell | southbound | swinging |
| sensible | souvenir | switch |
| sequels | sparkle | swore |
| sequence | sparklers | sympathy |
| session | spell | |
| sewage | spheres | taxes |
| sexual | spicy | television |
| sharp | spore | teller |
| shelf | spread | thankful |
| shelves | spreadsheet | theatrical |
| ship | stable | their |
| shipped | staff | thematic |
| shipping | stall | therapist |
| shiver | starchy | therapy |
| shook | stationary | there |
| shoplifter | stationery | thermometer |
| shorten | steady | thermostat |
| shoulder | stern | they |
| sigh | stitch | they're |
| sight | stood | thief |
| simplification | store | thieves |
| site | stormy | thimble |
| sixteenth | stylish | thinking |
| sixty | subconscious | thirsty |
| sketch | subcontract | thirteenth |
| skinnier | submit | thirty |
| sleigh | submitted | thorough |
| slippers | subsidiary | though |

threw

through

thumb

tomato

tomatoes

took

torrential

touchpad

tough

toughen

tragedy

transferable

transfusion

transmission

transportation

tray

trays

trio

triumphant

trouble

turkey

turkeys

unbreakable

union

uplift

upset

ushers

utterance

vacation

vacationer

valiant

variation

varied

varies

vary

vegetable

vertical

veto

vetoes

video

vision

vitamin

voiceless

volleyball

waist

waited

walnut

waltz

waste

watch

water

wealth

wear

weather

wedge

Wednesday

weight

weightlifter

wheel

wheezing

whenever

where

whether

whey

whimsical

whine

whirlpool

whisper

white

whitewash

who

whole

wholesale

wholesome

whom

whose

wicker

William

winning

witch

wood

woodpecker

wool

word

work

workshop

world

worldwide

worm

worry

worse

worship

worth

worthwhile

wrapper

wrestling

wrinkle

wrist

wristband

write

writer

young

youth

zero

zeroes

## SPELLING DEMONS

The following words are frequently misspelled. Compile a list of words that are **your** spelling demons—words that seem to give you trouble all the time. Are these some of yours?

| | | |
|---|---|---|
| affect | elicit | occasional |
| amateur | embarrass | occurrence |
| angel | environment | omitted |
| angle | familiar | opinion |
| apparatus | February | petal |
| brilliant | governor | playwright |
| clothes | height | prejudice |
| cough | heroine | professor |
| cylinder | judgment | recommend |
| definite | library | religious |
| doughnut | nausea | separate |
| effect | nickel | vacuum |